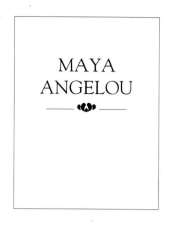

MAYA
ANGELOU

MAYA ANGELOU

Miles Shapiro

CHELSEA HOUSE PUBLISHERS
New York   Philadelphia

Chelsea House Publishers
Editorial Director Richard Rennert
Executive Managing Editor Karyn Gullen Browne
Copy Chief Robin James
Picture Editor Adrian G. Allen
Art Director Robert Mitchell
Manufacturing Director Gerald Levine
Production Coordinator Marie Claire Cebrián-Ume

Black Americans of Achievement
Senior Editor Sean Dolan

Staff for MAYA ANGELOU
Editorial Assistant Joy Sanchez
Assistant Designer John Infantino
Picture Researcher Wendy P. Wills
Cover Illustrator Daniel O'Leary

First Printing

1 3 5 7 9 8 6 4 2

Library of Congress Cataloging-in-Publication Data
Shapiro, Miles.
    Maya Angelou: author / Miles Shapiro.
      p. cm.—(Black Americans of achievement)
    Includes bibliographical references and index.
Summary: Discusses the life and work of the noted black writer.
        ISBN   0-7910-1891-1.
                0-7910-1862-8 (pbk.)
  1. Angelou, Maya—Biography—Juvenile literature.
2. Afro-American women authors—20th century—Biography
—Juvenile literature. [1. Angelou, Maya. 2. Authors, American.
3. Afro-Americans—Biography] I. Title. II. Series.
PS3551.N464Z87 1993   93-3249
818'.5409—dc20   CIP
[B]   AC

Frontispiece: *Maya Angelou in
1971 with a copy of what remains
her best-known work,* I Know Why
the Caged Bird Sings.

CONTENTS

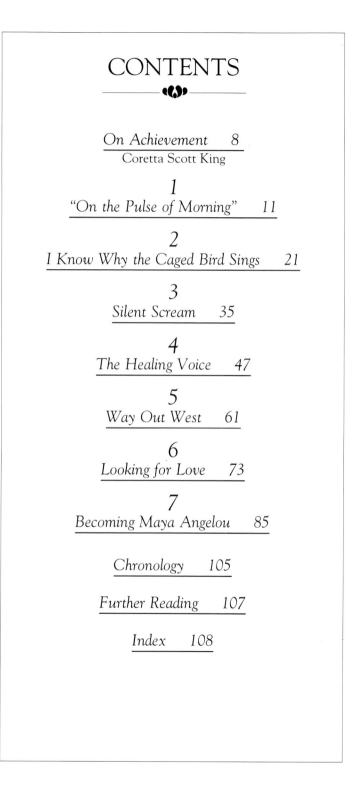

BLACK AMERICANS OF ACHIEVEMENT

HENRY AARON
baseball great

KAREEM ABDUL-JABBAR
basketball great

RALPH ABERNATHY
civil rights leader

ALVIN AILEY
choreographer

MUHAMMAD ALI
heavyweight champion

RICHARD ALLEN
*religious leader and
social activist*

MAYA ANGELOU
author

LOUIS ARMSTRONG
musician

ARTHUR ASHE
tennis great

JOSEPHINE BAKER
entertainer

JAMES BALDWIN
author

BENJAMIN BANNEKER
scientist and mathematician

AMIRI BARAKA
poet and playwright

COUNT BASIE
bandleader and composer

ROMARE BEARDEN
artist

JAMES BECKWOURTH
frontiersman

MARY MCLEOD BETHUNE
educator

JULIAN BOND
civil rights leader and politician

GWENDOLYN BROOKS
poet

JIM BROWN
football great

RALPH BUNCHE
diplomat

STOKELY CARMICHAEL
civil rights leader

GEORGE WASHINGTON
CARVER
botanist

RAY CHARLES
musician

CHARLES CHESNUTT
author

JOHN COLTRANE
musician

BILL COSBY
entertainer

PAUL CUFFE
merchant and abolitionist

COUNTEE CULLEN
poet

BENJAMIN DAVIS, SR., AND
BENJAMIN DAVIS, JR.
military leaders

SAMMY DAVIS, JR.
entertainer

FATHER DIVINE
religious leader

FREDERICK DOUGLASS
abolitionist editor

CHARLES DREW
physician

W. E. B. DU BOIS
scholar and activist

PAUL LAURENCE DUNBAR
poet

KATHERINE DUNHAM
dancer and choreographer

DUKE ELLINGTON
bandleader and composer

RALPH ELLISON
author

JULIUS ERVING
basketball great

JAMES FARMER
civil rights leader

ELLA FITZGERALD
singer

MARCUS GARVEY
black nationalist leader

JOSH GIBSON
baseball great

DIZZY GILLESPIE
musician

WHOOPI GOLDBERG
entertainer

ALEX HALEY
author

PRINCE HALL
social reformer

MATTHEW HENSON
explorer

CHESTER HIMES
author

BILLIE HOLIDAY
singer

LENA HORNE
entertainer

LANGSTON HUGHES
poet

ZORA NEALE HURSTON
author

JESSE JACKSON
civil rights leader and politician

MICHAEL JACKSON
entertainer

JACK JOHNSON
heavyweight champion

JAMES WELDON JOHNSON
author

MAGIC JOHNSON
basketball great

SCOTT JOPLIN
composer

BARBARA JORDAN
politician

MICHAEL JORDAN
basketball great

CORETTA SCOTT KING
civil rights leader

MARTIN LUTHER KING, JR.
civil rights leader

LEWIS LATIMER
scientist

SPIKE LEE
filmmaker

CARL LEWIS
champion athlete

JOE LOUIS
heavyweight champion

RONALD MCNAIR
astronaut

MALCOLM X
militant black leader

THURGOOD MARSHALL
Supreme Court justice

TONI MORRISON
author

ELIJAH MUHAMMAD
religious leader

EDDIE MURPHY
entertainer

JESSE OWENS
champion athlete

SATCHEL PAIGE
baseball great

CHARLIE PARKER
musician

GORDON PARKS
photographer

ROSA PARKS
civil rights leader

SIDNEY POITIER
actor

ADAM CLAYTON
POWELL, JR.
political leader

COLIN POWELL
military leader

LEONTYNE PRICE
opera singer

A. PHILIP RANDOLPH
labor leader

PAUL ROBESON
singer and actor

JACKIE ROBINSON
baseball great

DIANA ROSS
entertainer

BILL RUSSELL
basketball great

JOHN RUSSWURM
publisher

SOJOURNER TRUTH
antislavery activist

HARRIET TUBMAN
antislavery activist

NAT TURNER
slave revolt leader

DENMARK VESEY
slave revolt leader

ALICE WALKER
author

MADAM C. J. WALKER
entrepreneur

BOOKER T. WASHINGTON
educator and racial spokesman

IDA WELLS-BARNETT
civil rights leader

WALTER WHITE
civil rights leader

OPRAH WINFREY
entertainer

STEVIE WONDER
musician

RICHARD WRIGHT
author

ON ACHIEVEMENT

Coretta Scott King

BEFORE YOU BEGIN this book, I hope you will ask yourself what the word *excellence* means to you. I think that it's a question we should all ask, and keep asking as we grow older and change. Because the truest answer to it should never change. When you think of excellence, perhaps you think of success at work; or of becoming wealthy; or meeting the right person, getting married, and having a good family life.

Those important goals are worth striving for, but there is a better way to look at excellence. As Martin Luther King, Jr., said in one of his last sermons, "I want you to be first in love. I want you to be first in moral excellence. I want you to be first in generosity. If you want to be important, wonderful. If you want to be great, wonderful. But recognize that he who is greatest among you shall be your servant."

My husband, Martin Luther King, Jr., knew that the true meaning of achievement is service. When I met him, in 1952, he was already ordained as a Baptist preacher and was working toward a doctoral degree at Boston University. I was studying at the New England Conservatory and dreamed of accomplishments in music. We married a year later, and after I graduated the following year we moved to Montgomery, Alabama. We didn't know it then, but our notions of achievement were about to undergo a dramatic change.

You may have read or heard about what happened next. What began with the boycott of a local bus line grew into a national movement, and by the time he was assassinated in 1968 my husband had fashioned a black movement powerful enough to shatter forever the practice of racial segregation. What you may not have read about is where he got his method for resisting injustice without compromising his religious beliefs.

He adopted the strategy of nonviolence from a man of a different race, who lived in a different country, and even practiced a different religion. The man was Mahatma Gandhi, the great leader of India, who devoted his life to serving humanity in the spirit of love and nonviolence. It was in these principles that Martin discovered his method for social reform. More than anything else, those two principles were the key to his achievements.

This book is about black Americans who served society through the excellence of their achievements. It forms a part of the rich history of black men and women in America—a history of stunning accomplishments in every field of human endeavor, from literature and art to science, industry, education, diplomacy, athletics, jurisprudence, even polar exploration.

Not all of the people in this history had the same ideals, but I think you will find something that all of them had in common. Like Martin Luther King, Jr., they all decided to become "drum majors" and serve humanity. In that principle—whether it was expressed in books, inventions, or song—they found something outside themselves to use as a goal and a guide. Something that showed them a way to serve others, instead of only living for themselves.

Reading the stories of these courageous men and women not only helps us discover the principles that we will use to guide our own lives but also teaches us about our black heritage and about America itself. It is crucial for us to know the heroes and heroines of our history and to realize that the price we paid in our struggle for equality in America was dear. But we must also understand that we have gotten as far as we have partly because America's democratic system and ideals made it possible.

We are still struggling with racism and prejudice. But the great men and women in this series are a tribute to the spirit of our democratic ideals and the system in which they have flourished. And that makes their stories special and worth knowing.

1
"ON THE PULSE
OF MORNING"

"**I** HADN'T SO much forgot as I couldn't bring myself to remember" was how she began her own story, with the long-buried memory of a painful incident from her childhood: one Easter Sunday in the 1930s, in front of the assembled congregation of the Colored Methodist Episcopal Church in Stamps, a rigidly segregated small town on the Red River in Lafayette County in the southwest corner of Arkansas, she was unable to remember the words of a poem she was to recite, to the great amusement of her friends and schoolmates and her ultimate humiliation.

Proud, intelligent, introspective, and sensitive, young Marguerite Johnson had long felt like an outsider in Stamps, set apart by her unwillingness to speak with a southern accent, use "common slang," or eat soul food. Teased often about the way she looked—she later remembered "all the things they said about 'my daddy must of been a Chinaman' (I thought they meant made out of china, like a cup) because my eyes were so small and squinty"—she fantasized that she was different, better, because of a secret that only she knew: "I was really white . . . a cruel fairy stepmother, who was understandably jealous of my beauty, had turned me into a too-big Negro girl, with nappy black hair, broad feet and a space between her teeth that would hold a number-two pencil."

January 20, 1993: From the west steps of the Capitol, Maya Angelou reads her poem "On the Pulse of Morning" for the inauguration of President Bill Clinton.

Easter Sunday, the feast of resurrection and re-birth, was to be the day that Marguerite revealed her true self to the world. In the lavender silk taffeta dress that her grandmother, Annie Henderson (Marguerite and her beloved brother Bailey called her Momma), had made for her, she would look beautiful and glamorous, an exotic creature, not a misfit, a swan, not an ugly duckling, and those who had teased her and made fun of her would plead for her friendship and beg forgiveness for their insults. "I was going to look like one of the sweet little white girls who were everybody's dream of what was right with the world," she later wrote. "When people saw me wearing it they were going to run up to me and say, 'Marguerite [sometimes it was 'dear Marguerite'], forgive us, please, we didn't know who you were,' and I would answer generously, 'No, you couldn't have known. Of course I forgive you.' . . . Wouldn't they be surprised when one day I woke out of my black ugly dream, and my real hair, which was long and blond, would take the place of the kinky mass that Momma wouldn't let me straighten?"

But Easter brought instead the first of many disillusionments for Marguerite Johnson. In the truthful light of the morning sun, the dress of which she had been so proud looked garish and grotesque, "a plain ugly cut-down from a white woman's once-was-purple throwaway." It was too long, she now thought, like an old woman's dress, and even so did not sufficiently hide her endless skinny legs, which were coated with dust from the red Arkansas clay by the time she finished walking to the church. "Everyone in church," she thought as she stood to recite her Easter poem, "was looking at my skinny legs." Forgetfulness set in, and it seemed she could not take in enough of the hot still air "to breathe out shame," and she fled the church, to an even greater embarrassment.

"I hadn't so much forgot as I couldn't bring myself to remember. Other things were too important." The sentences refer not just to young Marguerite Johnson's failure to recall the rhymes of a childish Easter poem, but to her struggle, as a mature woman and artist known to the world as Maya Angelou, to give shape and sense and beauty in words to a life that had been filled with an overwhelming diversity of experience, much of it sorrowful, some of it tragic, some of it improbable, some of it exhilarating, all of it fascinating—a searing, profound, and ultimately joyful lesson in the consequences of being an independent black woman in 20th-century America. Maya Angelou's incredible odyssey had taken her from the stifling safety of Momma's general store in Stamps to the big cities of St. Louis and San Francisco, from strip clubs to the world's most glamorous stages, from the rural American South to Mother Africa. She had been, along the way, a sexually abused little girl traumatized into silence, unwed teenage mother, streetcar conductor, wife, stripper, prostitute, madame, dancer, short-order cook, songwriter, singer, civil rights activist, actress, dramatist, journalist, and teacher. For much of this time, other things had been too important for her to bring herself to remember; she had been too busy living her life, supporting herself and a child, to take time to ponder its meaning. Perhaps, too, there was much that she preferred to forget.

But the written word had often been her consolation in times of loneliness—"all those years in that little town in Arkansas, I learned through the literature," she once said—and in the late 1950s she became determined to be a writer. Baited by Robert Loomis, an editor at Random House—"he told me it was almost impossible to write autobiography as literature and I probably couldn't do it anyway"—the ever-fearless and willful Angelou began the lonesome and frightening work of shaping her memories into a coherent and compelling narrative. "I hadn't so much forgot as I couldn't bring myself to remember" was the first sentence she gave herself as author in the first of her five (to date) autobiographical volumes, *I Know Why the Caged Bird Sings*. Though the books chart an incredible journey from a legacy of oppression, hatred, and hurt to self-awareness and understanding, the process of memory has indeed often proved painful. "It's still scary every time I go back to the past," Angelou told an interviewer in 1982. "Each morning my heart catches. When I get there, I remember how the light was, where the draft was coming from, what odors were in the air. When I write, I get all the weeping out." She described the act of writing as "dragging my pencil across the old scars to sharpen it."

The five volumes of autobiography (*I Know Why the Caged Bird Sings*, which was published in 1970

Clinton repeats the oath of office to Chief Justice of the Supreme Court William Rehnquist as his wife, Hillary (right), and daughter, Chelsea (left), look on. Clinton said that he chose Angelou to read at his inauguration because she "embodies a spirit of hope and unity that is quintessentially American."

was followed by *Gather Together in My Name* in 1974, *Singin' and Swingin' and Gettin' Merry Like Christmas* in 1976, *The Heart of a Woman* in 1981, and *All God's Children Need Traveling Shoes* in 1986; Angelou has also published four volumes of poetry) have not finished her story, however, for they conclude before she made her resolution to tell her life and so do not convey the acclaim that followed in the wake of their publication. The words of essayist and novelist James Baldwin, the foremost black writer of his generation, epitomize a more general reaction to Angelou's work: "This testimony from a Black sister marks the beginning of a new era in the minds and hearts and lives of all Black men and women. . . . *I Know Why the Caged Bird Sings* liberates the reader into life simply because Maya Angelou confronts her own life with such a moving wonder, such a luminous dignity. I have no words for this achievement, but I know that not since the days of my childhood, when the people in books were more real than the people one saw every day, have I found myself so moved. Her portrait is a Biblical study of life in the midst of death."

And by bringing herself to remember, Maya Angelou brought herself, on the sunny winter Wednesday of January 20, 1993, to a place that no African American, and no woman, and only one poet before her had ever been. In the shadow of the Capitol in Washington, D.C., with thousands of her fellow Americans gathered to watch and listen and millions more present via television and radio, Maya Angelou read aloud a poem of her own composition to accompany the inauguration of her fellow Arkansan, Bill Clinton, as the 42nd president of the United States. Clinton had been born and raised in Hope, Arkansas, some 20 miles north of Stamps in Hempstead County; he had asked Angelou to read a poem for his inauguration because her life and work seemed to embody his brightest hopes for his administration: an America in which individual potential triumphs over poverty, neglect, and racism; a nation cognizant of the sins of its past, but ready to forgive, and to be forgiven; a hopeful society, informed by its history but looking forward, with a place in it for all the diverse individuals who have made and continue to shape it in the search for that elusive salvation called the American Dream.

Deeply honored but made nervous by the enormity of what she was about to undertake, in the weeks leading up to the inauguration Angelou had repeatedly asked her fellow Americans to pray for her as she worked on her poem. To somehow articulate the hopes and fears of her compatriots at this particular juncture in their nation's history, not with the shopworn rhetoric and exhortations of political speech making but with the subtle magic of poetry, was a tremendous—some would even say foolhardy—task. But this time, reading in her rich, melodious, beautifully cadenced voice, Maya Angelou did not forget or falter.

Entitled "On the Pulse of Morning," her poem was itself an act of memory. In 665 words, she summoned the memories of all those ("The Asian, the Hispanic, the Jew/The African, the Native American/The Sioux/The Catholic, the Muslim, the French, the Greek/The Irish, the Rabbi, the Priest, the Sheik/The Gay, the Straight, the Preacher/The privileged, the homeless, the teacher") who have sought and continue to seek on this American land a new beginning and escape from a history hopefully more cruel than their future, as well as those—the poet's ancestors, among them "the Ashanti, the Yoruba, the Kru"— come here unwillingly, in contradiction of America's promise, from freedom to slavery. "Each of you," she told her listeners, is the "descendant of some passed-on traveller"; "each of you," she read, is "a bordered country/Delicate and strangely made proud." She related as well the memories of the American land itself, left by "armed struggles for profit" and the depredations of "seekers desperate for gain" and "starving for gold" with "collars of waste" upon its shore and "currents of debris upon [its] breast."

It was a dark vision of American history, perhaps, but one suffused nonetheless with hope. It had its parallel, in that regard, with the poet's own history—a chain of specific events that might have broken a different person, a series of general circumstances, such as poverty and racial oppression, that had condemned many people like her, but which she had managed to overcome in order to reach a point where she could look with optimism toward the future. "What I'm interested in is *survival*," Angelou told an interviewer in 1973. "But not just bare, awful, plodding survival. Survival with some *style*, some faith. . . . I love stories about survival, I'm thrilled by them, enchanted."

And like all great literature, her story moves from the individual to the general; the story of her own survival, some of it still unwritten and culminating in her appearance at the inauguration, contains the seeds of hope for the survival and betterment of all those like her. In her work, Angelou told an interviewer in 1985, "I use the first person singular, [but] I'm talking about the third person plural all the time; what it's like to be a human being. So the person who reads my work and suspects that he or she knows me, hasn't gotten the half of the book, because he or she should know himself or herself better after reading my work. That's my prayer." As singular and desperate as some of her experiences had been, for Angelou they were reason not for alienation but for closer communion with the rest of humankind. "I am talking about *all* people," she said in 1987. "I'm always talking about the human condition. So, if it's possible for me, Maya Angelou, me, myself to feel thirst then I know it's possible for you to feel thirst. And if my tongue dries up with thirst, then I know how your tongue must feel when there's no liquid. . . . I accept that we human beings are more alike than unalike and it is

The new president and his favorite living poet embrace following Angelou's recital. For all her achievements, Angelou has a simple means of assessing her contributions: "I'd just like to be thought of as someone who tried to be a blessing rather than a curse to the human race."

that *similarity* that I talk about all the time. Yes, not just surviving . . . but thriving with passion and compassion, and humor and style, and excitement and glory, and generosity and kindness." The basic theme of her work, she has said, is "the refusal of the human spirit to be hardened . . . the persistence of innocence against all obstacles."

On that chilly, sun-drenched January morning in the nation's capital, she urged her fellow citizens to bring themselves to remember. "History, despite its wrenching pain/Cannot be unlived, but if faced/With courage, need not be lived again," Maya Angelou said to a nation facing its gravest economic crisis since the Great Depression, a nation in which it seemed that the racial and economic divisions between its citizens—inescapable legacies from the past—had never been greater, a nation that had seemingly been determined, for the previous 12 years, on an act of collective forgetting regarding the most troublesome problems of its past and present. But her painful past had taught Maya Angelou that each day is a new opportunity. One's foremost obligation, she had once said, is to "live life fully, fiercely, devotedly. . . . All we're trying to do is to get from birth to death. And you can't fail. Even if you only live five minutes, you've succeeded. . . . And the scars that you can't help but acquire can be truly marks of beauty."

"Lift up your eyes upon/This day breaking for you," Maya Angelou encouraged all those who listened to her at the inauguration; "Give birth again/To the dream." "I am inspired when I see this country in light of the other countries in the world," Angelou said in 1977. "To think that this country, which was literally built upon the slaughter of human beings, still believes in the dream of 'the land of the free and the home of the brave,' is an incredible thing. It may take hundreds, or perhaps thousands of years to realize, but to dream it, just to dream it, is in itself an elevating experience."

By bringing herself to remember, Maya Angelou had created, in her work and in her person, an example of infinite possibility and promise for others. "Women, children, men," she read, urging her nation to make a journey similar to her own, "Take [this day] into the palm of your hands/Mold it into the shape of your most/Private need. Sculpt it into/The image of your most public self./Lift up your hearts/Each hour holds new chances/For a new beginning." By remembering her past, Maya Angelou had been able to create her future. "Your passages have been paid," she now read; "Lift up your faces, you have a piercing need/For this bright morning dawning for you. . . . Here, on the pulse of this new day/You may have the grace to look up and out/And into your sister's eyes, and into/Your brother's face, your country/And say simply/Very simply/With hope—/Good morning."

2

I KNOW WHY
THE CAGED BIRD SINGS

WHAT THE WORLD knows of the remarkable life of Maya Angelou is largely what she has told her readers, beginning with *I Know Why the Caged Bird Sings*, the first of her five autobiographies, "a carefully wrought, simultaneously touching and comic memoir . . . whose beauty is not in the story but the telling," according to Christopher Lehmann-Haupt, book reviewer of the *New York Times*. This combination of seriousness and laughter would be characteristic of Angelou's work and life. When asked in 1973 by interviewer Bill Moyers what advice she would give a young black woman growing up, she responded, "I would say you might encounter many defeats but you must never be defeated, ever. In fact it might even be necessary to confront defeat. It might be necessary to get over it, all the way through it, and go on. I would teach her to laugh a lot. Laugh a lot at the—at the silliest things and be very, very serious."

Some critics have wondered whether Angelou's autobiographies might more properly be classified as autobiographical novels in that, in exercising the power of her imagination, Angelou sometimes, in the words of one reader, "mixes fact with fantasy." But the writer, Angelou points out, must sometimes distinguish between the truth and facts.

"There's a world of difference between truth and facts," she said in 1989. "Facts can obscure the truth. You can tell so many facts that you fill the stage but haven't got one iota of truth." Although in this way her books would seem to function more like fiction, which uses invented events to tell truths about the

A black child hoes a field in the rural South at the height of the Great Depression. At the time, the majority of the blacks in the United States still lived in the South and earned their livelihood through agriculture, most often as tenant farmers, sharecroppers, or migrant workers on land owned by whites.

human condition, Angelou insists that her works should be classified as autobiographies, not autobiographical novels. "They are autobiographies," she said in 1983. "When I wrote *I Know Why the Caged Bird Sings*, I wasn't thinking so much about my own life or identity. I was thinking about a particular time in which I lived and the influences of that time on a number of people. I kept thinking, what about that time? What were the people around young Maya doing? I used the central figure—myself—as a focus to show how one person can make it through those times."

In so doing, she hoped to accomplish something unique in American literature, as she explained in 1975: "There are very few American writers who use the autobiographical form for their literary output almost exclusively. I hope to look through my life at life. I want to use what has happened to me—what is happening to me—to see what human beings are like, to tell anecdotes so true, to look behind the fact of the anecdote and see what motivated this person in this action, and that person, so that people who have never known blacks—or Americans, for that matter—can read a work of mine and say, you know, that's the truth."

Chronologically, her story begins with rejection. "When I was three and Bailey four," she wrote, "we had arrived in the musty little town, wearing tags on our wrists which instructed—'To Whom It May Concern'—that we were Marguerite and Bailey Johnson Jr., from Long Beach, California, en route to Stamps, Arkansas, c/o Mrs. Annie Henderson." The two youngsters had been put on a train cross-country, with their tickets pinned to Bailey's inside coat pocket, bound for the home of their paternal grandmother following the most recent and final bust-up of their parents' "calamitous" marriage. Years later, the writer remembered little of the journey except for the kindness of black strangers, who, accustomed to traveling with packed lunch boxes because of the uncertainty in the segregated South of finding establishments that would serve them, plied the little wayfarers with fried chicken and potato salad.

Marguerite Johnson had been born in St. Louis, Missouri, on April 4, 1928, which makes the year of her momentous train trip 1931 or 1932. The nation was about to enter the gravest years of the Great Depression, though the effects of that economic disaster on the population of Stamps would be felt slowly. Most of the blacks in Stamps lived such a precarious economic existence to begin with that, initially at least, the depression was not of great consequence to them. "The Depression must have hit the white section of Stamps with cyclonic impact," Angelou wrote, "but it seeped into the black area slowly, like a thief with misgivings. The country had been in the throes of the Depression for two years before the Negroes in Stamps knew it. I think that everyone thought that the Depression, like every-thing else, was for the whitefolks, so it had nothing to do with them. Our people had lived off the land and counted on cotton-picking and hoeing and chop-ping seasons to bring in the cash needed to buy shoes, clothes, books and light farm equipment. It was when the owners of cotton fields dropped the payment of ten cents for a pound of cotton to eight, seven and finally five that the Negro community realized that the Depression, at least, did not discriminate."

The Johnson children's grandmother, Annie Henderson, whom Maya and Bailey called Momma, enjoyed a somewhat more secure existence than many of the black residents of Stamps. Mrs. Hender-son owned and operated a general store, the Wm. Johnson General Merchandise Store, behind which she lived with her grown son, Willie Johnson, and, after their unannounced arrival, her two grand-children, who were the offspring of her other son, Bailey Johnson. Mrs. Henderson had been married three times. Her first husband, William Johnson, had lent his name to the store and fathered William and Bailey before disappearing. Her second husband Maya never met and knew only as Mr. Henderson; her attempts to gather more information about him were firmly rebuffed by her grandmother, who "never answered questions directly put to her on any subject except religion." The third, Mr. Murphy, was a shadowy figure Maya met only once; that day, she recalled later, was the only Sunday she ever knew her Uncle Willie to stay home from church. He missed services, he told her, to keep Mr. Murphy from "robbing them blind."

For Maya—the name was given her by her brother as a shortened version of "my sister"—the Store ("it was always spoken of with a capital s") quickly became her "favorite place to be. Alone and empty in the mornings, it looked like an unopened present from a stranger." There, its clientele could buy any-thing from needles and thread to chicken feed and hog mash, coal oil and light bulbs (for those privileged enough to afford electricity), lard, flour, salt, mackerel, salmon, and tobacco. Mrs. Henderson had begun her business early in the 20th century as the operator of a lunch wagon that sold food and lemonade to the workers at the lumber mill and cotton gin that constituted Stamps's two industries. After a short time, she used her profits to build the Store, which soon became a kind of social and business center for the black section of Stamps. Women came there to exchange gossip as well as to shop; on Saturdays, barbers cut hair on the Store's porch and itinerant musicians sang the blues. Momma was one of the very few blacks in Stamps to own her own business and land; most of her customers were the black field hands who arrived early in the

morning, before the sun was up, to make five-cent purchases before boarding the trucks that would carry them to the white people's cotton fields. Boastful and optimistic at the break of day, they would disembark from the trucks at the end of the day beaten down and disenchanted. "Brought back to the Store, the pickers would step out of the backs of the trucks and fold down, dirt-disappointed, to the ground. No matter how much they had picked, it wasn't enough. Their wages wouldn't even get them out of debt to my grandmother, not to mention the staggering bill that waited on them at the white commissary downtown."

Despite her relative success, Momma, like the rest of Stamps's black population, could not escape the South's system of racial and economic oppression.

Along with the cotton gin, the lumber mill (pictured) in Stamps was one of the small town's only two industries. The economy of Stamps, like that of most small towns in the South, was dependent on the land and what it could sustain.

Stamps, said its black residents, was a town so prejudiced that blacks were not even allowed to buy vanilla ice cream—except on the Fourth of July. Otherwise, it had better be chocolate. Although blacks sometimes joked that the Great Depression did not really affect them because their economic status in the United States was such that they had always been in a depression, hard times in Stamps ultimately proved catastrophic for its black population, as the already criminal wages paid for picking cotton dwindled to next to nothing. Because her customers now had no money at all with which to pay their bills, Momma Henderson's business suffered accordingly. Characteristically, she improvised a solution. Various relief agencies provided the poor people of Stamps with lard, flour, salt, powdered eggs, and powdered milk, which Momma soon began accepting in trade in lieu of cash. As a result, although her family was one of the few in town not on relief, Maya and Bailey "were the only children in the town proper that we knew who ate the powdered eggs every day and drank the powdered milk," which they hated. Sometimes, they dropped in on one of the poorer families just to be able to eat crackers and peanut butter, which the family would have obtained in exchange for its relief rations.

Hard times were easier for Maya to comprehend and bear than was the South's code governing race relations. Maya found it difficult to understand, for example, why her grandmother, a woman of enormous dignity and immense physical presence— "People spoke of Momma as a good-looking woman and some, who remembered her youth, said she used to be right pretty. I saw only her power and strength. She was taller than any woman in my personal world, and her hands were so large they could span my head from ear to ear. Her voice was soft only because she chose to keep it so."—should have to

endure in stoic silence the taunts and indignities of the "powhitetrash" (poor white trash) children whose families lived on Momma's land.

But for blacks in Stamps, as elsewhere in the South, the penalty for noncompliance with its racial codes could be dire. Poverty and economic dependence kept most blacks "in their place," but the underpinning of the entire system was violence and terror, as Maya and Bailey would soon learn. One evening not long after Bailey and Maya arrived in Stamps, the sheriff visited the Store for the purpose of advising Momma that her son, Maya's Uncle Willie, "better lay low tonight" because "some of the boys'll be coming over here later." The "boys" were the white-robed members of the local Ku Klux Klan, who were making one of their periodic nocturnal

A railroad station in the segregated South at the beginning of the Great Depression. Blacks and whites entered the station by separate doors, bought tickets at separate counters, waited for their trains in separate waiting rooms, and sat in separate cars while traveling to their destinations.

A rally of the Ku Klux Klan in Mississippi during the 1920s. The Klan was founded by white southerners in 1866, just after the defeat of the South in the Civil War. Its initial purpose was to terrorize the freed black slaves of the South into claiming none of the economic and political rights newly granted them.

forays. The cause of their prowling was ostensibly a sexual transgression committed by a black man against a white woman, but their real mission was simply to instill fear in the heart of Stamps's blacks, and every black male they came across, not just the alleged culprit, was at risk of being lynched. Uncle Willie, a gentle, sensitive fellow whose twisted physique (he resembled a giant Z, Maya wrote) and halting gait—the result of a childhood accident—made him the butt of many jokes by the Store's customers, was made to lie in hiding all night at the bottom of a bin filled with potatoes and onions for fear of the Klansmen. Much later, Bailey would witness a much more horrifying example of the methods used by whites to protect their dominant economic and social position.

Momma Henderson endured such assaults to the mind and spirit with dignity and an abiding religious faith. ("During the picking season my grandmother would get out of bed at four o'clock . . . and creak down to her knees and chant in a sleep-filled voice, 'Our Father, thank you for letting me see this New Day. Thank you that you didn't allow the bed I lay on last night to be my cooling board, nor my blanket my winding sheet. Guide my feet this day along the straight and narrow, and help me to put a bridle on my tongue. Bless this house, and everybody in it.'") For her, the various indignities and insults blacks were made to suffer were simply part of the way things were. To challenge the established order of things was to risk injury and even death, which was something she was not about to let her grandchildren do.

"Momma intended to teach Bailey and me to use the paths of life that she and her generation and all the Negroes gone before had found, and found to be good ones," Maya wrote many years later. "She didn't cotton at all to the idea that white folks could be talked to at all without risking one's life. And certainly they couldn't be spoken to insolently. In fact, even in their absence they could not be spoken of too harshly unless we used the sobriquet 'They.' If she had been asked and had chosen to answer the question of whether she was cowardly or not, she would have said that she was a realist."

Though more questioning and less accepting than her grandmother, Maya understood the fear that bound the town's blacks. She likened her and Bailey's twice-yearly ventures into the white part of town to buy fresh meat with which to supplement their diet of salt pork and canned greens and preserves—one thing the Store did not have was refrigeration—to "explorers walking without weapons into man-eating animals' territory." For Bailey and Maya, whites were mysterious (because unknown), fearsome (for their power and unpredictability), and enviable (for their wealth). "In Stamps," according to Angelou, "the segregation was so complete that most Black children didn't really, absolutely know what whites looked like. Other than that they were different, to be dreaded, and in that dread was included the hostility of the powerless against the powerful, the poor against the rich, the worker against the worked for and the ragged against the well dressed." She remembered, she wrote years later, "never believing that whites were really real. . . . Whitefolks couldn't be people because their feet were too small, their skin too white and see-throughy, and they didn't walk on the balls of their feet the way people did—they walked on their heels like horses.

"People were those who lived on my side of town. I didn't like them all, or, in fact, any of them very much, but they were people. These others, the strange pale creatures that lived in their alien unlife, weren't considered folks. They were whitefolks."

There were consolations among the hardship. Though Momma could be stern and had rigid ideas about the way children should behave—" 'Thou shall not be dirty' and 'Thou shall not be impudent' were the two commandments of Grandmother Henderson upon which hung our total salvation," Maya wrote, and impudence was defined so broadly as to include such offenses as looking an adult in the face—she was also loving and devoted to the well-being of her grandchildren. "Her world was bordered on all sides with work, duty, religion and 'her place,'" Maya wrote. "I don't think she ever knew that a deep-brooding love hung over everything she touched." From her, Maya learned "common sense, practicality and the ability to control one's own destiny that comes from constant hard work and courage." The young girl was also secure in the love of her brother, Bailey, "the greatest person in my world." Though always small for his age, he was handsome, smart, and a born leader, and he always looked out for his baby sister. When other adults made unkind comments about Marguerite's somewhat ungainly looks, about which she was very sensitive—"I was big, elbowy and grating," she wrote—Bailey, who "was small, graceful and smooth," always sprang to her defense. In private moments, he reassured her that she was beautiful.

There was also the Store, where Marguerite felt safe and secure and where "weighing the half-pounds of flour [or mash, meal, sugar or corn], excluding the scoop, and depositing them dust-free into the thin paper sacks held a simple kind of adventure." When she was right, and the measure she had poured out on the scale caused the needle to stop just where it should and the appreciative customers crowed, "Sister Henderson sure got some smart grand-childrens," she rewarded herself with a chocolate kiss. When the needle stopped short of the measure requested, and the customers cackled, "Put some more in that sack, child. Don't you try to make your profit offa me," she punished herself with no chocolate. At night, Momma, Marguerite, Bailey, and Uncle Willie would sit down in the back of the store to simple suppers of crackers, sliced onions, and canned sardines. "In the evening, when we were alone like that, Uncle Willie didn't stutter or shake or give any indication that he had an 'affliction.' It seemed that the peace of a day's ending was an assurance that the covenant God made with children, Negroes and the crippled was still in effect."

Esther Rolle, as Annie Henderson, and Constance Good, as Marguerite "Maya" Johnson, in a scene from the television movie of I Know Why the Caged Bird Sings *in 1979. This particular scene was set in the Store, which Maya described as initially seeming to her and Bailey like a "Fun House of Things where the attendant had gone home for life."*

Black field hands relax on the porch of a store after receiving their wages. Such scenes were a common sight throughout the South on payday. "On Saturdays," Angelou wrote in I Know Why the Caged Bird Sings, *"barbers sat their customers in the shade on the porch of the Store, and troubadours on their ceaseless crawlings through the South leaned across its benches and sang their sad songs of the Brazos while they played juice harps and cigar-box guitars."*

Most of all, there was the consolation that so many lonesome children have taken refuge in—books. Marguerite and Bailey were both prodigious readers at a young age, and when customers came to call at the store, they often had to rap at the counter to engage the attention of the girl, who was usually so engrossed in her reading that she did not even notice them come in. With her "young and loyal passion," she loved the works of such black American writers as Paul Laurence Dunbar, Langston Hughes, James Weldon Johnson, and W. E. B. Du Bois, but her true favorite was William Shakespeare, her "first white love," especially his 29th sonnet. Though she felt somewhat guilty about her fondness for Shakespeare's poetry, because he was white—"I pacified myself about his whiteness by saying that after all he had been dead so long it couldn't matter to anyone any more"—Sonnet 29 seemed to beautifully and perfectly express the deep and pervading loneliness she felt as a black, which in Stamps, as elsewhere in the South and indeed in the United States, was to be a despised, second-class citizen, and as a young girl without her parents. "When in disgrace with fortune and men's eyes," it begins, "I all alone beweep my outcast state/And trouble deaf heaven with my bootless cries/And look upon myself and curse my fate."

For all Momma's love for Marguerite and Bailey could not make up for the absence of their parents. Trying to create a reality that was more palatable than the knowledge that her parents had essentially abandoned them, Marguerite had convinced herself that her mother and father had died, but that belief was shattered one Christmas when she received gifts from her parents—a tea set and a blue-eyed, blond-haired doll from her mother, and a photograph of himself from her father. Bailey, too, received presents, and the effect on both children was devastating. Instead of joy, the gifts brought only sorrow, as the two cried and cried and wondered what they had done so wrong to make their parents send them away. Momma's scolding for their ungratefulness did little to make them feel better. Finally, after several days, Bailey convinced his sister that the gifts from their mother meant that she was intending to come get them. "Maybe she had just been angry at something we had done, but was forgiving us and would send for us soon," Bailey said. So the children tore Marguerite's doll to pieces, and then they waited. ❧

3

SILENT SCREAM
❧

WHEN MAYA WAS seven and Bailey eight, their waiting ended. Without any advance notice, their father, Bailey Johnson, Sr., pulled into Stamps one morning in a big gray De Soto. Big, handsome, well dressed, and extremely well spoken, he was nonetheless not quite what Maya had envisioned. "He had the air of a man who did not believe what he heard or what he himself was saying," and his daughter sensed that his newfound interest in his children was less than genuine. He was self-absorbed, and his attempts at humor sometimes came at his daughter's and his crippled brother's expense. When, after three weeks, he announced that he had to return to California (where he worked as a hotel doorman and then as a dietician for the navy), Maya, like her grand-mother, was relieved. Unlike Bailey, who had re-sponded positively, she did not want to reply to her father's insistent question: "Does Daddy's baby want to go to California with Daddy?"

Without ever really deciding, Maya found herself in the back of her father's De Soto—the two Baileys rode up front—with suitcases and boxes on the long road out of Stamps. In a short time, Maya grew suspicious. How did they even know this was really their father? What if they were being kidnapped? "For all I knew," Maya remembered later, "we were being driven to Hell and our father was the delivering devil." She demanded that he take her back to Stamps. Her fears turned to terror when in reply he asked, "You mean Daddy's baby doesn't want to go to St. Louis to see her mother? She's not going to eat you up, you know."

Diahann Carroll (right) played Vivian Baxter, Maya's mother, in the television film of I Know Why the Caged Bird Sings. *Though initially insensitive to her young daughter's needs, Vivian ultimately proved an excellent mother to Maya.*

The little girl began crying, heedless of Bailey's solace. The rejection she had known was better than facing some new, face-to-face hurt. What if their mother turned out to be like their father, vain and selfish, and laughed at them, she wondered. What if she had other children that she preferred to them? Guilt mingled with fear as Maya wondered why she did not feel more excited about meeting the woman she and her brother always referred to as Mother Dear. Her father only worsened the situation by asking, in reference to her tears, "What do you think your mother will say, when I tell her her children don't want to see her? . . . What will she say to that?"

"To describe my mother," wrote Maya years later, "would be to write about a hurricane in its perfect power. Or the climbing, falling colors of the rainbow." In the living room of her maternal grandmother's home in St. Louis, Maya was literally struck dumb at the first sight of her mother. If her father had been something less than Maya had hoped for, Vivian Baxter was something out of a dream—beautiful, glamorous, and mysterious, with an aura of danger and power surrounding her. "My mother's beauty literally assailed me. Her red lips (Momma said it was a sin to wear lipstick) split to show even white teeth and her fresh-butter color looked see-through clean. Her smile widened her mouth beyond her cheeks beyond her ears and seemingly through the walls to the street outside. . . . I knew immediately why she had sent me away. She was too beautiful to have children. I had never seen a woman as pretty as she who was called 'Mother.'" Though Maya had a harder time forgetting the sense of abandonment and rejection she had known, Bailey "fell instantly and forever in love. I saw his eyes shining like hers; he had forgotten the loneliness and the nights when we had cried together because we were 'unwanted children.'"

Vivian Baxter, known as Bibbie to friends and family, was a member of an insular and unusual clan, extraordinary in its "meanness" and mutual devotion. Her mother, a nurse by training, was a "nearly white" woman of mixed ancestry who spoke with a guttural German accent (she had been raised by a German family) and commanded enormous respect in the black section of St. Louis as a precinct captain, which meant that she had connections and influence with the police department, city government, and the courts that allowed her to bestow various important favors on the needy—get someone a city job, for example; or keep the heat off illegal gambling parlors; or obtain the release of an individual from jail. In exchange, she expected unquestioning loyalty to the political candidates of her designation at election time.

St. Louis (or at least the black section of town) at the time was, as it had been through much of its history, a freewheeling river city with "all the finesse of a gold-rush town." Every manner of illegal activity seemed to flourish there, "so obliviously practiced," wrote Maya Angelou, "that it was hard for me to believe that they were against the law." Raffish characters of every description—numbers runners, gamblers, and dealers in various illicit products— could be seen going to and fro on their various errands or "[hanging] around in front of saloons like unhorsed cowboys." They could also be seen, quiet and respect- ful, hats in hand, waiting silently in the Baxter living room for Grandmother Baxter when Maya and Bailey came home from school in the afternoon. "The men in their flashy suits and fleshy scars sat with churchlike decorum and waited to ask favors from her. . . . They knew what would be expected of them. Come election, they were to bring in the votes from the neighborhood. She most often got them leniency, and they always brought in the vote."

Grandfather Baxter was a black immigrant from the West Indies. The Baxter family's famous devotion to one another started with him; "Bah Jesus [by

A motorcycle division of the St. Louis police department amasses in front of the city's Jefferson Memorial. Her clout with the police made Maya's Grandmother Baxter an important person in their St. Louis neighborhood.

Jesus]," he would say, "I live for my wife, my children and my dog." There were six of those children, but it was Maya's uncles Tutti, Tom, and Ira who were the most renowned for their "unrelenting meanness,"

a quality in which they were encouraged by their father. "Bah Jesus," he would thunder, "if you ever get in jail for stealing or some such foolishness, I'll let you rot. But if you're arrested for fighting, I'll sell the house, lock, stock, and barrel, to get you out!" His sons took him at their word. Maya admitted later to being "thrilled by their meanness. They beat up whites and Blacks with the same abandon, and liked each other so much that they never needed to learn the art of making outside friends."

Vivian Baxter was "the only warm spirit among them," according to her daughter, but she could be a rough customer as well; the time she beat with a billy club a self-styled tough guy who had made the mistake of cursing her had become an oft-told family legend. Like her mother, Vivian was a nurse by training, but she more often made her living by running illegal card games, an occupation for which she was unapologetic. She never cheated anyone, she later told her children, her living was as honest (and often more lucrative) than most available to black women, and she liked surviving by her wits. Besides which, she enjoyed the night life.

For the first six months after their arrival in St. Louis, Maya and Bailey lived with their grandparents while their mother prepared a home for them. The big city offered a whole new variety of experiences for the youngsters from Stamps. There were the various operators and hustlers on the streets and in Grandmother Baxter's living room; there were new treats for the taste buds, such as thin-sliced German ham eaten in sandwiches rather than country style and jelly beans eaten from a bag with peanuts, which soon replaced chocolate kisses in Maya's affection and were, in her opinion, the "best thing the big town had to offer." There were the taverns, especially Louie's, where Vivian plied her trade and sometimes brought her children in the afternoon to eat boiled shrimp and drink soda pop while she danced—"like a pretty kite that floated just above my head"—to slow blues from the jukebox. Here, too, she taught her children how to dance, though it would be many

years, Maya wrote, "before I found the joy and freedom of dancing well."

For all the strangeness of the city—"I had decided that St. Louis was a foreign country"—there were ways in which the newcomers found themselves much more advanced than their presumably more sophisticated urban counterparts. Despite the impressiveness of the Toussaint L'Ouverture Grammar School itself, where the children were enrolled, Maya and Bailey were stunned by "the ignorance of our schoolmates," who "were shockingly backward," and by the "rudeness of our teachers."

Having become wizards at arithmetic from all the counting and calculation necessary to work in the Store, and having become masterful readers "because in Stamps there wasn't anything else to do," Maya and Bailey were skipped ahead a grade so as not to embarrass their less precocious fellow students. Even so, they remained amazed at the city children's lack of knowledge, and Bailey took great delight in taunting the bigger kids on the playground with such

Maya's mother, Vivian Baxter, made her living running illegal card games in saloons such as this one. "[Bootlegging], gambling, and their related vocations were so obviously practiced that it was hard for me to believe they were against the law," Angelou wrote about St. Louis in I Know Why the Caged Bird Sings.

questions as "who was Napoleon Bonaparte" and "how many feet make a mile." Her teachers Maya found to be pretentious and remote. It was a year before she heard anything from them that she had not already heard before.

After six months, the Johnson children moved in with their mother. For Bailey, Vivian Baxter could do no wrong, but Maya was still somewhat wary, feeling an unspoken threat that if she did something that her mother did not like, she would be sent back to Stamps. Her fear of such a fate made her dull-witted and slow, as if any movement, statement, or even thought might constitute the necessary offense.

Vivian Baxter lived with a companion, a man the children knew only as Mr. Freeman, who worked as a foreman for the Southern Pacific Railroad. Completely enthralled by the fun-loving, beautiful Vivian Baxter, Freeman treated her children, for the most part, with benign neglect. He "moved gracefully, like a big brown bear, and seldom spoke to us," Maya wrote. At night, after he returned home from work, he waited up for Vivian to return from her business. "He simply waited for Mother and put his whole self into the waiting. He never read the paper or patted his foot to radio. He simply waited. That was all." It was only when Vivian arrived home that Freeman came alive; from their bedrooms, the two children would hear the clink of glasses, music from the radio, and what sounded like the shuffle of Vivian's feet as she danced.

Maya would later claim that moving from place to place "meant absolutely nothing" to her. "It was simply a small pattern in the grand design of our lives," she wrote. "If other children didn't move so much, it just went to show that our lives were fated to be different from everyone else's in the world." Even so, it is clear that the children felt some sense of dislocation, as manifested by various symptoms

"You see, I'm often asked: 'How did you escape it all, the poverty, the rape at an early age, a broken home, growing up black in the South?' My natural response is to say: 'How the hell do you know I did escape? You don't know what demons I wrestle with.'" So spoke Maya Angelou to an interviewer in 1973, one year before this photograph was taken.

that began to display themselves at this time. Bailey's rapid-fire speech began to be slowed by a stutter, and Maya experienced terrifying nightmares. To soothe her, Vivian began the habit of allowing her little girl to sleep in her bed with herself and Mr. Freeman.

One morning, Maya awoke to find herself alone in the bed with Mr. Freeman. Speaking softly to her, he touched her and then pulled her on top of him as he gratified himself sexually. Confused and frightened, Maya, who had known little physical affection, was nonetheless grateful for the closeness the encounter provided: "Then came the nice part. He held me so softly that I wished he wouldn't ever let me go. I felt at home. From the way he was holding me I knew he'd never let me go or let anything bad happen to me. This was probably my real father and we had found each other at last. But then he rolled over, leaving me in a wet place, and stood up."

Immediately afterward and for weeks following, Freeman was brusque and distant with the girl, who was not quite sure what she had done wrong. "If you ever tell anybody what we did, I'll have to kill Bailey," he told her. Maya "began to feel lonely for Mr. Freeman and the encasement of his big arms," and then it happened again. For months afterward, the man did not speak to the girl, who "was hurt and for a time lonelier than ever." But soon, armed with her first library card, she lost herself in a world of books and stories that "became more real to me than our house, our mother, our school or Mr. Freeman." Then he raped her.

The badly injured girl confessed what had happened to Bailey, who, fortunately for Freeman, told Grandmother Baxter, who had the man arrested before he experienced the wrath of the children's uncles. At his trial, Maya was asked by the defense attorney if the rape was the first time Freeman had touched her. Very confused and feeling guilty—"Mr. Freeman had surely done something wrong, but I was convinced that I had helped him do it"—Maya nonetheless realized that if she answered yes, the defense attorney would somehow twist her answer to make her appear somehow culpable for the crime that had been committed against her, and her mother and grandmother and uncles would be very disappointed in her. So the little girl lied, and she answered no.

"The fact that I arrived at my desired destination by lies made it less appealing to me," she wrote years later. Freeman was convicted and given a sentence of a year and a day but somehow managed to obtain his release that very afternoon. In a couple of hours, a policeman arrived at Grandmother Baxter's, where Bailey and Maya were seeking to divert themselves with a game of Monopoly, with the announcement that Freeman had been found stomped to death in a vacant lot near the slaughterhouse.

The news shocked Maya into silence. In her mixture of confusion, guilt, and hurt, she concluded that it was her lie that was responsible for the man's death, and she decided that she had to stop speaking, so that no one else could be harmed by her words. "Instinctively, or somehow, I knew . . . if I talked to anyone else that person might die too." She resolved to remain silent, except with Bailey, and she became withdrawn and virtually mute. Her St. Louis family tolerated this behavior for what they regarded as a reasonable amount of time, until they thought she had had sufficient time to recover, but "when I refused to be the child they knew and accepted me to be, I was called impudent and my muteness sullenness. For a while I was punished for being so uppity that I wouldn't speak; and then came the thrashings, given by any relative who felt himself offended." In a very short time, Maya and Bailey found themselves on the train back to Stamps. ❧

4

THE HEALING VOICE

THOUGH THE FAMILIARITY of Stamps was most welcome to Maya, the sleepy town initially offered acceptance, not healing. Wounded and terrorized in various ways themselves, Stamps's black inhabitants accepted the silent little girl as she was, without calling attention to her condition. Such acceptance was kind, and perhaps necessary for the girl at first, but it did little to speed the painful work of healing. "The barrenness of Stamps was exactly what I wanted," she later wrote. "After St. Louis, with its noise and activity, its trucks and buses, and loud family gatherings, I welcomed the obscure lanes and lonely bungalows set back deep in dirt yards. The resignation of its inhabitants encouraged me to relax. They showed me a contentment based on the belief that nothing more was coming to them, although a great deal more was due. Their decision to be satisfied with life's inequities was a lesson for me. . . . Nothing more could happen, for in Stamps nothing could happen."

While Bailey amused himself by telling sarcastic, tongue-in-cheek tales of life in the big city to the curious customers at the Store—"everybody wears new clothes and have inside toilets. If you fall down in one of them, you get flushed away into the Mississippi River"—Maya remained silent. Even so, the returned children became minor celebrities in Stamps as a result of their trip, which was treated as a fabulous adventure. Because the "high spots in Stamps were usually negative: droughts, floods, lynchings and deaths. . . . farmers and maids, cooks

"You can't use up creativity," Maya Angelou, seen here as she was photographed in 1975, has said on many occasions. "The more you use, the more you have. Sadly, too often creativity is smothered rather than nurtured." Her own creativity was first encouraged in Stamps by a remarkable woman named Bertha Flowers.

and handymen, carpenters and all the children in town made regular pilgrimages to the Store" in order "just to see the travelers."

Deeply hurt by having been made to leave his mother again, Bailey nonetheless treated his sister with exceptional kindness; the anger that he vented in his cruel put-ons of the unsophisticated townspeople was nowhere in evidence in his dealings with Maya. Momma, too, and Uncle Willie (both of whom were aware of what had happened to her) were sympathetic, as were, for different reasons, the townspeople: "People, except Momma and Uncle Willie, accepted my unwillingness to talk as a natural outgrowth of a reluctant return to the South. And as an indication that I was pining for the high times we had had in the big city. Then, too, I was well known for being 'tender-hearted.' Southern Negroes used that term to mean sensitive and tended to look upon a person with that affliction as being a little sick or in delicate health. So I was not so much forgiven as I was understood."

Despite such understanding, Maya continued to withdraw, to the point where she began to wonder if she was going mad. The world outside seemed slightly unreal and out of focus; colors seemed faded, voices muffled, and she had difficulty attaching names to faces. Except for a select few individuals—Momma, Uncle Willie, and Bailey—all the people and things around her seemed to constitute one vague, blurred, faintly oppressive mass, of which she took no particular notice in the hope that it would take no specific notice of her and she would be spared further hurt. "For nearly a year," she wrote, "I sopped around the house, the Store, the school and the church, like an old biscuit, dirty and inedible." But someone had taken notice of her and her troubles—two wise old women: her grandmother and Mrs. Bertha Flowers.

To the black people of Stamps, and especially to young Marguerite Johnson, Bertha Flowers was the paragon of beauty, grace, and accomplishment, an "aristocrat . . . our side's answer to the richest white woman in town." With her imperturbable dignity, elegant bearing, educated speech, "soft yet carrying voice," and "rich black" skin, to Maya she was "the measure of what a human being can be. . . . It would be safe to say she made me proud to be a Negro, just by being herself. She acted just as refined as whitefolks in the movies and books and she was more beautiful."

So elegant was Mrs. Flowers that Maya was embarrassed by her friendship with Grandmother Henderson. The determinedly silent girl cringed when her uneducated grandmother called out, with easy familiarity, "How you, Sister Flowers?" as her friend passed by on the road in front of the Store, and she hung her head in shame at Momma's grammatical errors when the two women got together to gossip. If Mrs. Flowers's style and grace made Maya proud to be black, they also made her ashamed of her roots.

One day, Mrs. Flowers stopped by the Store to purchase a few items. In seeming deference to her social status, Grandmother Henderson volunteered to have Bailey carry her groceries up the road to her house, but Mrs. Flowers demurred. "Thank you, Mrs. Henderson," she replied. "I'd prefer Marguerite, though. . . . I've been meaning to talk to her, anyway." With that, the two women exchanged a meaningful glance, and at her grandmother's instructions Maya burst inside to change into something appropriate for the rare honor of a visit to Mrs. Flowers's house. Further embarrassment for the girl followed when her grandmother, in response to Mrs. Flowers's praise of her ability as a seamstress—the dress Maya had changed into, like all the rest of the clothes she and Bailey wore, had been made by Momma—took the dress off of her in order to display some intricate stitching she had done around the arms. Mortified,

Maya "wouldn't look at either of them. Momma hadn't thought that taking off my dress in front of Mrs. Flowers would kill me stone dead. . . . Mrs. Flowers had known that I would be embarrassed and that was even worse. I picked up the groceries and went out to wait in the hot sunshine. It would be fitting if I got a sunstroke and died before they came outside."

The hurt little girl and the beautiful woman walked together along a smooth path beside the rutted road, the girl trailing sullenly behind until beckoned forward by a gentle request from Mrs. Flowers. The woman told Maya that she had heard that the girl was doing excellent written work in school, but that her teachers had trouble getting her to talk in class. "Now no one is going to make you talk," Mrs. Flowers said. "Possibly no one can. But bear in mind, language is man's way of communicating with his fellow man and it is language alone which separates him from the lower animals. . . . Your grandmother says you read a lot. Every chance you get. That's good, but not good enough. Words mean more than what is set down on paper. It takes the human voice to infuse them with the shades of deeper meaning." With that, Mrs. Flowers went on to say that she was going to lend Maya some books, and she wanted her to read them aloud, testing each sentence for all its infinite varieties of sound, nuance, and meaning.

In the older woman's immaculate house, the two sat down to a snack of fresh-baked butter cookies and lemonade over ice, while Mrs. Flowers imparted to the girl the first of what they later called "lessons in living." It was wrong of her, Mrs. Flowers explained, to be ashamed of seemingly simple country people like her grandmother. Some people were not intelligent, the graceful woman explained, while others were simply uneducated; "some people, unable to go

to school, were more educated and even more intelligent than college professors." She should be "in-
tolerant of ignorance but understanding of illiteracy,"
and she should pay attention to the wisdom of
country people and her elders. Many years later, Maya
would write, she realized that her grandmother and
Mrs. Flowers "were as alike as sisters, separated only
by formal education."

When they had finished their snack, Mrs. Flowers
took a book from her shelf and began reading aloud.
It was *A Tale of Two Cities* by the great 19th-century
British novelist Charles Dickens, a story of heroism
and sacrifice in the French Revolution, and as the
woman read aloud the book's famous opening passage—"It was the best of times, it was the worst of
times; it was the season of light, it was the season of
darkness"—it was as if, for all her reading, Maya was
just now understanding for the first time the magical,
mysterious power of words. "Yes, ma'am," the silent
girl responded when her new friend asked if she
had liked the reading. "It was the least I could do,"
she wrote later of this tentative reply, "but it was the
most also."

Soon she would be able to do more. Carrying
some books and a bag of cookies for Bailey, she ran
home excitedly, eager to begin memorizing a poem
to recite for Mrs. Flowers at their next lesson. In the
warmth of the older woman's attention, the girl was
reminded that kindness as well as cruelty exists in the
world. For the first time, Marguerite Johnson felt that
she had been singled out for attention not out of
obligation or cruelty, but because someone had taken
a liking to her. In this first experience of what it is
like to be told one is special, she reawakened to the
world. "I was liked, and what a difference it made,"
she wrote. "I was respected not as Mrs. Henderson's
grandchild or Bailey's sister but for just being Marguerite Johnson. Childhood's logic never asks to be

Black field hands take a lunch break away from the cotton fields in Arkansas in 1938. "When they tried to smile to carry off their tiredness as if it was nothing, the body did nothing to help the mind's attempt at disguise. Their shoulders drooped even as they laughed," Maya wrote about the cotton pickers who congregated in her grandmother's store at the end of every working day. To Maya, on her return from St. Louis, it seemed that nothing in Stamps ever changed.

proved. . . . I didn't question why Mrs. Flowers had singled me out for attention, nor did it occur to me that Momma might have asked her to give me a little talking to. All I cared about was that she had made tea cookies for *me* and read to *me* from her favorite book. It was enough to prove that she liked me."

But the South had many ways to crush the spirit of its young black men and women. At the age of 10, Maya went to work after school and on weekends in the kitchen of Mrs. Viola Cullinan, a fat white woman with pretensions of gentility. On learning that Maya's given name was Marguerite, one of Mrs. Cullinan's friends announced that she should refer to her new help as Mary instead, because Marguerite was too long a name. To Maya's dismay, Mrs. Cullinan indeed did begin to refer to her only by the shorter name—an unbearable insult in what it said about the white woman's utter contempt for the identity of her young black employee. In horror, Maya learned that the cook in the Cullinan household, an older black woman, had allowed herself to be similarly renamed 20 years earlier. Eight decades after the abolition of slavery, white southerners still felt free to strip blacks of their name and identity. "If growing up is painful for the Southern Black girl, being aware of her displacement is the rust on the razor that threatens the throat. It is an unnecessary insult," Maya wrote many years later.

In this situation, her elders were of little help to Maya. Momma was of a generation that, fearful of the consequences of resistance, responded to such insults with forbearance, but Bailey had a solution to his sister's dilemma. One day, Maya took Mrs. Cullinan's favorite dishes, and when the overbearing woman summoned her with a shout of "Mary!", she "accidentally" dropped them. Mrs. Cullinan dropped to the floor in tears and then began hurling pieces of broken crockery at the girl, who quickly fled, never to return.

There were other, vicarious victories among the cycle of hard work and poverty in black Stamps, where "weekdays resolved on a sameness wheel," resolving "themselves so steadily and inevitably that each seemed to be the original of yesterday's rough draft." In a scene that was enacted, with certain variations, throughout black America, the Store would fill with people each time the great black boxer, Joe Louis, who was the heavyweight champion of the world from 1937 to 1949, defended his title. As Uncle Willie tuned the radio and turned the volume as high as it would go, women, many of them carrying infants, sat down atop every available chair, barrel, or wooden crate, while the men leaned against shelves and counters and the children listened from the porch.

The broadcast of the fight crackled from the radio into a religious near-silence. Sales of merchandise

Denied most opportunities for economic and social achievement, blacks took great pride in the pugilistic achievements of Joe Louis, who reigned as heavyweight champion of the world from 1937 to 1949. In demonstrating his superiority in the ring, Louis became the embodiment of black aspirations.

were forbidden in the Store during the fight, as the ring of the cash register broke the solemn atmosphere. At stake was much more than the heavyweight championship of the world; the combatants were fighting to determine nothing less than the future of all black Americans. At those rare moments when the contender had Louis in trouble, "my race groaned," Maya wrote. "It was our people falling. It was another lynching, yet another Black man hanging on a tree. One more woman ambushed and raped. A Black boy whipped and maimed. It was hounds on the trail of a man running through slimy swamps. It was a white woman slapping her maid for being forgetful.

"The men in the Store stood away from the wall and at attention. Women greedily clutched the babes on their laps while on the porch the shufflings and smiles, flirtings and pinching of a few minutes before were gone. This might be the end of the world. If Joe lost we were back in slavery and beyond help. It would all be true, the accusations that we were lower types of human beings. Only a little higher than the apes. True that we were stupid and ugly and lazy and dirty and unlucky and, worst of all, that God Himself hated us and ordained us to be hewers of wood and drawers of water, forever and ever, world without end."

But the mood changed when, inevitably, Louis came off the ropes to punch his opponents into submission. With the end of the referee's count and his oft-repeated proclamation, "the winnah, and still heavyweight champeen of the world . . . Joe Louis," jubilation reigned in the Store. Shouts filled the air, people embraced, and the cash register rang again and again. "Champion of the world," Angelou wrote. "A Black boy. Some black mother's son. He was the strongest man in the world. People drank Coca-Colas like ambrosia and ate candy bars like Christmas.

Some of the men went behind the store and poured white lightning in their soft-drink bottles, and a few of the bigger boys followed them. Those who were not chased away came back blowing their breath in front of themselves like proud smokers.

"It would take an hour or more before the people would leave the Store and head for home. Those who lived too far had made arrangements to stay in town. It wouldn't do for a Black man and his family to be caught on a lonely country road on a night when Joe Louis had proved that we were the strongest people in the world."

But there were enemies and forces that even the heavyweight champion of the world could not vanquish. In 1940, Marguerite Johnson took her place as a member of the eighth-grade graduating class of Lafayette County Training School. She was one of the stellar students in that class and had not been absent or late even once. She took pride in her ability to recite the preamble to the U.S. Constitution faster than any of her classmates and even Bailey, and she could name all the presidents of the United States in chronological or alphabetical order. With academic

A jubilant crowd in Harlem, in New York City, celebrates Louis's 1938 victory over the German contender Max Schmeling. Like Jesse Owens's four gold medals at the 1936 Olympic Games, Louis's knockout of Schmeling was hailed by Americans as an athletic refutation of Adolf Hitler's theories of racial superiority—a bitter irony in that segregation and racial discrimination still prevailed in most places in the homeland of these two champion athletes.

accomplishment had come a greater sense of self-acceptance; she was no longer as sensitive about her appearance, and friendships, particularly with a shy, pretty girl named Louise Kendricks, had made her more confident and outgoing. "Youth and social approval allied themselves with me," she wrote years later, "and we trammelled memories of slights and insults. The wind of our swift passage remodeled my features. Lost tears were pounded to mud and then to dust. Years of withdrawal were brushed aside and left behind."

On the morning of the graduation, it seemed to Maya that the sun had never shone so beautifully, and that every tomorrow would be even more gorgeous. "In my robe and barefoot in the backyard, under cover of going to see about my new beans, I gave myself up to that gentle warmth and thanked God that no matter what evil I had done in my life He had allowed me to live to see this day," she remembered.

The ceremony itself soon put an end to such grateful optimism, when a local white politician took the stage as the graduation speaker. Taking pains to let his audience know that they ought to be thankful for his presence—he did not even take time to stay for the ceremony itself—he spoke of all the educational improvements that were in store for Stamps: new microscopes and chemistry equipment for the laboratory, a renowned artist as a new art instructor.

But such improvements were to be made at the Central School—the immaculate, ivy-colored structure, surrounded by a well-manicured lawn, hedges, and a tennis court, where the white children attended classes. For all-black Lafayette County Training School, with its two run-down buildings surrounded by dirt fields indistinguishable, in winter, from the surrounding farmland, there might soon be a paved rather than a dirt lot for the children to play on, the politician added as an afterthought, then went on to praise the handful of individuals from the school who had gone to play sports at various black universities. To Maya and her classmates, the man's message was clear: white children could legitimately aspire to be scientists and doctors and nurses and painters and artists, while black children could dream of becoming athletes. Those who failed could be like the majority of blacks in the South—"maids and farmers, handymen and washerwomen . . . anything higher that we aspired to was presumptuous." With the white man's words, "the proud graduating class of 1940 had dropped their heads. . . . The white kids were going to have a chance to become Galileos and Madame Curies and Edisons and Gauguins, and our boys (the girls weren't even in on it) would try to be Jesse Owenses and Joe Louises. Owens and the Brown Bomber were great heroes in our world, but what school official in the white-goddom of Little Rock [the state capital] had the right to decide that those two men must be our only heroes?"

With just a few words, the white politician had cast a long, dark shadow over a future that just that morning had stretched out before Maya so brightly. It is possible that, in his casual disregard for his listeners and unquestioning acceptance of segregation and its consequences, the man did not even realize how many hopes he had dashed, but other bigots were more overt.

Not long after graduation, Maya developed a crippling toothache—"excruciating penance for all the stolen Milky Ways, Mounds, Mr. Goodbars and Hersheys with Almonds"—that left her in such excruciating pain that "I prayed earnestly that I'd be allowed to sit under the house and have the building collapse on my left jaw." Everyday illnesses and aches took on an increased seriousness for the black population of Stamps. Much of rural America had few

The South's system of segregation meant that white schoolchildren invariably enjoyed the benefits of facilities and resources superior to those offered to their black counterparts.

physicians, dentists, and health-care professionals serving it, but the problem was compounded for black Americans in the South. Because of limited economic and educational opportunities, there were few black doctors or dentists, and many white physicians would not treat black patients.

There were no black dentists in Stamps. Grandmother Henderson had treated previous toothaches by either pulling the tooth (using a string tied to her fist), administering liberal doses of aspirin, or praying, but untreated cavities had left two of Maya's teeth rotted to the gums. The nearest black dentist was in Texarkana, 25 miles away—a long journey for a family without an automobile and with a child in excruciating pain. So Momma decided to bring Maya to see Dr. Lincoln, a white dentist in Stamps who, she said, owed her a favor. The dentist was just one of many people, white and black, to whom Mrs. Henderson had lent money during the depression.

Mrs. Henderson and Maya used the dirt path at the rear, on which black servants and tradespeople approached the Lincoln household, and knocked on the backdoor of the dentist's office. Tell the doctor Annie is here, she said to the white girl who answered the door, adhering to the southern code that dictated that in interchange with whites, blacks, no matter how distinguished or mature, were never Mister or Missus and had no last name. "The humiliation of hearing Momma describe herself as if she had no last name to the white girl was equal to the physical pain," Maya wrote. "It seemed terribly unfair to have a toothache and a headache and have to bear at the same time the heavy burden of Blackness."

The doctor kept them waiting in the hot sun for over an hour. My granddaughter has a toothache, Momma said to him in explaining her errand, using all the while an apologetic, subservient tone and increasing thereby Maya's anguish. "Annie, you

A black couple approaches the door of a "Colored Emergency Room" with their sick child. As Maya would learn, the practice of segregation in the South extended to the provision of health care, even in life-threatening circumstances.

know I don't treat nigra, colored people," he replied, whereupon Mrs. Henderson reminded him, ever so gently, of the favor he owed her. No, the dentist said, no. "I wouldn't press on you like this for myself but I can't take no," said Mrs. Henderson. "Not for my grandbaby."

"Annie," said the dentist, who had not so much as looked in the direction of the girl, "my policy is I'd rather stick my hand in a dog's mouth than in a nigger's." He went inside, followed, soon after, by the uninvited Mrs. Henderson, who shamed him into paying her the interest she had not originally charged him on his loan. Then the girl, dreaming retributive fantasies, and her grandmother rode the bus 25 miles to the "colored" dentist in Texarkana. ◆

5

WAY OUT WEST

❦

NOT LONG AFTER the incident with Dr. Lincoln, Momma Henderson informed her children that they would be going to California to be reunited with their parents. Maya never knew the exact reason for this newest migration; though her grandmother told her it was because she and Bailey had reached an age where they needed to be with their parents and that caring for them was getting to be too much for her in her old age, Maya suspected that her grandmother had other reasons. Her motivations were often inscrutable, Maya had observed; as was true of many of the black adults in Stamps, "her African-bush secretiveness and suspiciousness had been compounded by slavery and confirmed by centuries of promises made and promises broken." Such inscrutability, Maya recognized, had been developed as a means of self-protection, and in *I Know Why the Caged Bird Sings* she quoted an African-American aphorism that pertained to Momma's caution: "If you ask a Negro where he's been, he'll tell you where he's going."

Maya always suspected that there were other reasons for her departure from Stamps than the ones her grandmother provided. With Maya and Bailey reaching their teenage years, Momma in all likelihood recognized that both of them, with their lively intelligence and questioning nature, possessed the kind of spirit that was unlikely to easily make the types of accommodation with the South's racial codes necessary to ensure their safety. Unwilling to see either their spirits broken or their bodies violated,

Market Street in San Francisco in 1942. Wartime brought prosperity and jobs to San Francisco, and during World War II many blacks moved there to find work.

she decided to remove them from the scene of their utmost danger.

It was perhaps Bailey for whom Momma was most afraid. "The Black woman in the South who raised sons, grandsons and nephews had her heart-strings tied to a hanging noose," Maya wrote in explanation of her grandmother's fears, which were confirmed by an experience of Bailey's that his sister subsequently came to regard as critical in determining their departure.

One day, having been sent on an errand to the white part of Stamps, Bailey returned to the Store ashen and shaken. Repeated queries from Uncle Willie as to what was the matter brought no response. The child's silence was frustrating to the grown-ups, but his sister understood, in a way: "I knew when I saw him that it would be useless to ask anything while he was in that state. It meant that he had seen or heard of something so ugly or frightening that he was paralyzed as a result. He explained when we were smaller that when things were very bad his soul just crawled behind his heart and curled up and went to sleep."

What Bailey had seen on his way back from town was a variation on a traditional southern horror: a group of black men, at the direction of a grinning white man, retrieving the corpse of a black man from a pond. The corpse was bloated and rotten and wrapped in a sheet; the man had been lynched, and his genitals had been cut off. "This here's one nigger nobody got to worry about no more. He ain't going nowhere else," the white man said before ordering the blacks, the terrified Bailey among them, to carry the corpse into the nearby jail. Once they were inside, the white man barred the door and pretended he was not going to let Bailey out, while the prisoners screamed that they "didn't want no dead nigger in there with them." "Surely we ain't done nothing bad

enough for you to put another nigger in here with us, and a dead one at that," they said to the white man, whom they addressed as "Boss." "Then they laughed," Maya many years later quoted Bailey as saying. "They all laughed like there was something funny."

"He was away in a mystery," Maya wrote about her brother, "locked in the enigma that young Southern Black boys start to unravel, start to *try* to unravel, from seven years old to death. The humorless puzzle of inequality and hate." For Bailey's repeated question of why white people hated blacks so much, his grandmother and uncle had no answer, but that same night, Maya believed, her grandmother began to plan how to remove them to California. For young

A lynch mob admires its handiwork in Boston, Georgia, in 1936. Lynching was one method used by white southerners to intimidate blacks and keep them from protesting against the various inequities of southern life. Between the 1880s and the 1960s, more than 3,000 blacks were lynched in the South.

black men in the South, Maya wrote, their "very life depended on . . . not truly understanding the enigma." Bailey, frightened as he was, was too intelligent to ever cease trying to apprehend the mystery, so his grandmother hoped he would be safer elsewhere.

After brief stays in Los Angeles and Oakland, where most of the Baxter clan had relocated, Maya and Bailey moved in with their mother and her new husband, a successful businessman the children knew as Daddy Clidell, in a fourteen-room house on Post Street in the Fillmore district of San Francisco. The Fillmore area had previously been the center for San Francisco's large population of Japanese immigrants and their descendants, but with the outbreak of World War II these Japanese Americans were interned in prison camps by the federal government, which was suspicious of their loyalty now that Japan had become a declared enemy of the United States. In a short time the Japanese population of Fillmore was replaced by blacks, many of them lured to the big city from rural areas by the ready availability of jobs in various industries rejuvenated by the war, such as shipping and munitions manufacture. For blacks in San Francisco, as in many other urban areas in the United States, the war meant a period of relative prosperity, and for 24 hours a day the Fillmore district was a bustling hive of activity, filled with churches, gambling houses, all-night restaurants, saloons, shoe-shine parlors, and greasy spoons.

For Maya, the scene at her mother's house was just as exotic. Vivian Baxter was just as beautiful, just as independent, just as tough—in an incident that preceded the arrival of her children, she had twice shot, but not killed, a man who had made the mistake of calling her a "bitch"—and just as fearless as ever, and she had lost none of her affinity for the raffish side of life. With the help of Daddy Clidell, she supported her children "efficiently with humor and

Under armed guard, a small Japanese-American boy, perched atop his parents' luggage, awaits removal from San Francisco in April 1942. Because they were considered security risks, hundreds of Japanese Americans were deported from the city and sent to internment camps shortly after the outbreak of World War II.

imagination." The home on Post Street was made into a boardinghouse and was constantly echoing with the comings and goings of her lodgers, whom Maya found to be a fascinating cast of characters. There were shipyard workers, prostitutes, restaurateurs, and college students, as well as an unending stream of Daddy Clidell's friends. Boasting names like Stonewall Jimmy, Just Black, Cool Clyde, Tight Coat, and Red Leg, they were "the most colorful characters in the Black underground . . . the most successful con men in the world."

This was a happy time for Maya. For her, San Francisco "was a state of beauty and a state of freedom." Her academic prowess continued; she was

"To me, a thirteen-year-old Black girl, stalled by the South and Southern Black life style, the city was a state of beauty and a state of freedom," Angelou wrote in I Know Why the Caged Bird Sings. *"I became dauntless and free of fears, intoxicated by the physical fact of San Francisco."*

skipped ahead two semesters upon her arrival from Stamps, and at George Washington High School, inspired by a teacher named Miss Kirwin ("that rare educator who was in love with information"), she excelled. She also won a scholarship for evening classes at the California Labor School, where she

studied drama and, more important, dance. ("The only two things I've ever loved in my life are dancing and writing," she would tell an interviewer in 1988.)

Education of a different kind took place at home. Maya's experience with her mother's companions had left her warily prepared to ignore Daddy Clidell, but,

Reminiscing in 1982, Angelou recalled a conversation with her mother that influenced her greatly. "Baby, let me tell you something," Vivian Baxter said to her daughter, then a struggling young woman uncertain what direction her life would take. "I think you are the greatest woman I have ever met. . . .you are intelligent and merciful. Those two things don't often go together." Maya thought to herself: "She's not a liar; she's much too fierce to lie. She's intelligent, so maybe she sees something."

she soon discovered, "his character beckoned and elicited admiration." He possessed an irresistible combination of "strength lined with tenderness" and was that rarest of individuals, "a man of honor." With no children of his own, Daddy Clidell quickly grew very fond and proud of Maya, who so resembled him physically that, to his great delight, his friends often said to him, "Clidell, that's sure your daughter. Ain't no way you can deny her." "During the age when Mother was exposing us to certain facts of life," Maya remembered later, "like personal hygiene, proper posture, table manners, good restaurants and tipping practices, Daddy Clidell taught me to play poker, blackjack, tonk and high, low, Jick, Jack and the Game." The mental gymnastics required to play cards Maya found "marvelous for the brain."

Remarkably, Maya harbored little bitterness toward her mother for past rejections or for the horrible thing that had taken place in her home. Her mother, Maya acknowledged later, "was a poor mother for a child" in that "she did not know what to do with kids, except feed us and things like that," but as Maya grew toward adulthood, her relationship with Vivian Baxter deepened. Now the daughter was better able to understand the spirit and independence of her mother, who was fond of proclaiming "they spell my name W-o-m-a-n" and who steeled Maya to self-reliance with such aphorisms as "you may not always get what you pay for, but you will surely pay for what you get." Though their relationship would still have its ups and downs, Maya was coming to see her mother as supportive and wise, and Vivian was learning that there were things besides material comfort and shelter that she could give her daughter. In time, Maya would come to regard her mother as "one of the greatest human beings I've ever met," and much of her own philosophy is derived from her mother's approach. "Life is going to give you just what you put in it. Put your whole heart in everything you do, and pray, then you can wait," Vivian Baxter often told her daughter. "She comprehended the perversity of life, that in the struggle lies the joy," Maya later wrote.

Bailey Johnson, Sr., had less to offer his daughter. One summer, he invited Maya to spend her vacation from school with him at his home near San Diego. Maya "secretly expected him to live in a manor house surrounded by grounds and serviced by a liveried staff," but she arrived to find him ensconced in a trailer with a haughty young girlfriend, Dolores Stockland. To the great amusement of Bailey, Sr., who "seemed positively diabolic in his enjoyment of our discomfort," Maya and Dolores, who had expected, based on what she had been told, her beau's daughter to be a cute little girl of eight, not a nearly six-foot teenager, took an immediate dislike to one another.

Their mutual animosity came to a head after Bailey took his daughter with him on one of his periodic excursions across the Mexican border to a little cantina he frequented near Ensenada. There, Maya's father enjoyed the favors of a local admirer and guzzled tequila and beer until he passed out in the backseat of his Hudson. Though she had never driven a car before, Maya then took it upon herself to drive the more than 50 miles back home, but their trip was halted when she crashed the Hudson into another vehicle at a border checkpoint. Rousing himself from his stupor, Bailey used his considerable charm to extricate them from the situation.

But Dolores was not as forgiving as the border guards. Angered by her lover's antics, she accused him of letting his children interfere with their relationship, whereupon Bailey—putting words in his daughter's mouth—told her that Maya had been right when she had called her a "pretentious little bitch."

He then stormed from the trailer, leaving the two female combatants alone. An exchange of insults led inevitably to a fistfight and then an attempted assault by Dolores with a hammer. When Bailey returned home, he took his daughter to spend the night with some friends until he could restore the peace, but the next morning, while these friends were out, she ran away.

Maya spent the next several weeks in a junkyard, where she slept in an abandoned automobile and became the newest member of an egalitarian, multi-racial commune of young ragamuffins who survived by mowing lawns, scavenging glass bottles, and doing assorted odd jobs. In their easy camaraderie and unquestioning friendship, Maya felt accepted as never before. "After hunting down unbroken bottles and selling them with a white girl from Missouri, a Mexican girl from Los Angeles and a Black girl from Oklahoma, I was never again to sense myself so solidly outside the pale of the human race. The lack of criticism evidenced by our ad hoc community in-fluenced me, and set a tone of tolerance for my life." But the junkyard was refuge, not a home, and after a month she called her mother and asked her to send money for a flight to San Francisco. ◖◗

6

LOOKING FOR LOVE

HAVING EXPERIENCED A taste of being on her own, Maya had little desire to return to school when she got back to San Francisco. Her thirst for knowledge had not lessened any, but she was already a year ahead in her studies and she decided to take a job as a demonstration of her newfound self-reliance. With the headstrong determination—some would say impulsiveness—that would govern many of her adult actions, Maya determined not to take any of the typical jobs available for young black women without much education but to become a conductor on the city's streetcar line.

The main problem with this plan was that the Market Street Railway Company did not employ blacks. Undeterred by her mother's initial discouragement, the stonewalling of company officials, and the disinterest of civil rights organizations in her cause, Maya simply returned to the company's offices day after day until, at last, she was given a job application to fill out. Her lies about her age and experience (she added four years to her true age of 15) proved as convincing as her stubbornness, and she was hired as a conductor. "For one whole semester the streetcars and I shimmied up and scooted down the sheer hills of San Francisco," she wrote, and she greatly enjoyed the feeling of independence that her own income and bank account gave her. Vivian Baxter was greatly impressed; it was during this period, Maya later wrote, that she and her mother took some of the most important steps "on the long path toward mutual adult admiration."

As a single mother with a child to support, Maya sometimes worked as an exotic dancer, as shown in this publicity photo from the early 1940s.

73

After a semester, Maya returned to her classes, but she found it difficult to readjust to school. Having lived a little as an adult, she now found her classmates childish and their concerns trivial. "I knew I knew very little," she later wrote, "but I was certain that the things I had yet to learn wouldn't be taught to me at George Washington High School."

One of the things the tall teenager wanted to learn about was sex. Confused by her growing sexual awareness, uncertain of her attractiveness, wanting a boyfriend but foolishly unable to believe that anyone would be interested in her, she decided to confront the mysteries of sex in a most direct—and somewhat unusual—fashion. Maya chose a handsome and pop-ular boy from a street near where she lived and, upon encountering him by chance on the street one night, bluntly asked him if he would like to have sex with her. The encounter that ensued was without affection (not to mention love), real intimacy, or physical pleasure; the two did not even speak a word, and both left immediately after the consummation of the act.

From this single loveless tryst was born, nine months later, Maya's son Clyde (known also as Guy). For eight months, Maya managed to conceal her pregnancy from her classmates and family. Daddy Clidell's initial reaction when she revealed her secret, on the night of her high-school graduation, was amazement, but Vivian Baxter quickly adjusted to the situation. "There was no overt or subtle condemnation" from her mother, Maya wrote. "She was Vivian Baxter Jackson. Hoping for the best, prepared for the worst and unsurprised by anything in between."

"Well, that's that," Maya quotes her as saying in *I Know Why the Caged Bird Sings*, which ends with the daughter being awoken by her mother to witness her newborn son sleeping peacefully at her side.

"See," Vivian says to her daughter, who has been afraid to handle or sleep with the baby for fear of accidentally hurting him, "you don't have to think about doing the right thing. If you're for doing the right thing, then you do it without thinking." She ended the book with the birth of her son, Maya later told an interviewer, because "I wanted to end it on a happy note. It was the best thing that ever happened to me."

The decisions she had made left Maya with no choice but to enter immediately the world of adulthood. Although she followed a somewhat un-conventional path in fulfillment of her new respon-sibilities, she shouldered those responsibilities willingly. Even so, she often found doing the right thing for herself and her son to be not as easy as her mother had stated, as she relates in *Gather Together in My Name*. To her mother's and Daddy Clidell's offer to take care of Clyde while she continued her education, Maya responded negatively; instead, driven by a mixture of pride and insecurity, she left her mother's big house, determined to find a job that would allow her to support her child.

With absolutely no experience but an aptitude for prevarication, she landed a job as a cook at the Creole Café. (She lied and answered yes when asked if she could cook Creole; an old lodger at her mother's house, a retired gambler named Papa Ford, explained that so long as she put onions, green peppers, and garlic into every dish she cooked there, she would do fine, which proved to be true.) The job enabled her to rent a room for herself and her baby, and for a while she believed herself to be all set: "I had a beautiful child, who laughed to see me, a job that I did well, a baby-sitter whom I trusted, and I was young and crazy as a road lizard. Surely this was making it." Then romance intervened, in the person of a thirty-one-year-old sailor named Charles (known also as

The Russian writers Leo Tolstoy (left) and Maksim Gorky were photographed together in 1900. At a dark time in her own life, Maya drew strength from the brooding, melancholy quality of Gorky's prose.

Curly), a regular at the café, whose good looks, kindness, and gentleness led Maya to fall desperately in love with him. It was a feeling he reciprocated, but after just two months he returned to his native New Orleans to marry his fiancée, as he had told Maya at the outset of their affair that he would.

Left bereft, at Bailey's suggestion (and with a generous cash gift provided by him) Maya decided to ease her heartbreak by relocating. She tried Los Angeles first, only to find her Baxter relatives not especially generous with offerings of assistance, and then continued southward to San Diego, where she found work as a cocktail waitress at the Hi Hat Club, a loud, smoky joint frequented by prostitutes, pimps, thieves, fences, gangsters, and the occasional sailor. By night, from six until two, she worked, envying the prostitutes for the attention paid them by the club's male patrons (but not for their manner of earning a living); by day she took classes in modern dance and played with Clyde, who was otherwise placed in the care of a baby-sitter. She kept up her reading as well, developing a special affinity for the great Russian writers of the late 19th and early 20th century: the brooding, haunted novelist Fyodor Dostoyevsky; the elegant stylist Ivan Turgenev; the master of the short story and dramatist Anton Chekhov; and her favorite, novelist and playwright Maksim Gorky, "the blackest, most dear, most despairing."

The "measured tempo" of this life grew more accelerated when Maya managed to talk her way into the ownership of a small brothel, but this escapade lasted only a short while before, frightened by the prospect of a police investigation, she fled San Diego in such a hurry that she left behind even the green Chrysler convertible she had purchased with her stable's earnings.

Her flight took her all the way back to Stamps, but she soon discovered, as another American writer of the South, Thomas Wolfe (whose work Maya admired), put it, that "you can't go home again." In her memory, Maya wrote, Stamps was "a place of light, shadow, sounds and entrancing odors," but the atmosphere there, as would be impressed upon her shortly, "was pressed down with the smell of old fears, and hates, and guilt."

Despite Grandmother Henderson's warm welcome, Maya quickly realized that she had outgrown Stamps's comforts. Old friends criticized her for pretensions and big-city airs, envied her for having broken away from the small town, and scorned her for returning. ("They want to be free, free from this town, and crackers, and farming, and yes-sirring and no-sirring," a more sympathetic acquaintance explained.) The condescension and arrogance of the whites of the town, with their complacent expectation of deference and servility, so enraged her that what Grandmother Henderson had long feared would happen (and what had inspired her originally to remove her grandchildren from the poisoned environment) at last took place: Maya fought back, by insulting a condescending white store clerk. News of her "showing out" beat her home from town, and her terrified grandmother, who had never hit her as a child, slapped her repeatedly, heedless of the young woman's protests that her insult had been a matter of "principle."

"You think 'cause you've been to California these crazy people won't kill you?" her grandmother shouted. "You think them lunatic cracker boys won't try to catch you in the road and violate you? You think because of your all-fired principle some of the men won't feel like putting their white sheets on and riding over here to stir up trouble? You do, you're wrong. Ain't nothing to protect you and us except the good Lord and some miles." That afternoon, Maya climbed with Clyde into a horse-drawn wagon and left Stamps for good.

She did not find a significantly greater degree of solace in San Francisco. Mother and child moved back in with Vivian Baxter, whose independence had led to a breakup with Daddy Clidell and tumultuous relations with various succeeding lovers. "For the passionate," Maya wrote about her mother, "joy and anger are experienced in equal proportions and possibly with equal anticipation. My mother's capacity to enjoy herself was vast and her rages were legendary.

Mother never instigated violence, but she was known not to edge an inch out of the way of its progress." When a boyfriend attempted to enforce a dictate at knifepoint, Vivian cut him with a razor. "You goddam right," she responded to his exclamation of surprise, "and you lucky I don't shoot you on top of it." Such incidents were not uncommon; "the sound of police and ambulance sirens whine through my childhood memory with dateless frequency," Maya wrote in *Gather Together in My Name,* but she regarded her mother's determination not to allow anyone to take advantage of her as admirable.

Bailey's habits were more worrisome. Now a waiter on the Southern Pacific Railroad, he had grown remote and alienated and spent most of his free time out of the house; though he was still handsome, "his fast speech, which used to stumble into a stutter with excitement, had slowed, and a songless monotone rasped out his meanings." Papa Ford provided Maya with the explanation for the changes in her beloved brother: Bailey was using heroin.

Maya's own situation was not a great deal happier. Her work as a cook at a succession of diners brought her little satisfaction, and though she delighted in the beauty and laughter of her son, she knew that she had to do more to secure her own and his future. An attempt to join the army in order to take advantage of the educational and home-owning benefits of the GI Bill resulted in a rejection when the military claimed that the California Labor School, where Maya had studied dance on scholarship just a couple of years earlier, was a communist front organization. A brief flash of small-time success as the female half of a local dance team came to nothing when her male counterpart returned to his former girlfriend and partner. Though Bailey got straight and got married and recovered much of his old personality, Maya

The saxophonists Lester Young (on tenor sax, second from left) and Charlie "Bird" Parker (on alto, at right) helped transform jazz from popular entertainment to a modern art form. Jazz is sometimes cited as the most important cultural contribution of black Americans.

began to dose her restlessness, confusion, and depression with marijuana, which helped not as much as the music from the jazz records she had begun to collect: Billie Holiday, Lester Young, and above all the brilliant young beboppers Dizzy Gillespie, Max Roach, Bud Powell, and Charlie Parker.

With few real options open to her, Maya decided to relocate once again, to Stockton, a farm town in the San Joaquin Valley, 80 miles east of San Francisco, where a friend of her mother's had promised her a job as a cook in a restaurant. Her job required her to work until midnight, so Clyde was sent to live with a baby-sitter. Maya visited him on her days off, but her visits grew less frequent once she fell in love with

L. D. Tolbrook, a smooth-talking, handsome older man who convinced her that he was a professional gambler, with a drug-addicted harridan for a wife whom he was about to leave. Tolbrook treated the young single mother kindly and gave her money to buy clothes for herself and things for her son, but inevitably, with the deepening of her devotion, came the sad story: he had had a disastrous night at the gaming tables and was now in debt, for a ruinous sum, to some murderous wise guys. He needed cash in a hurry, upon pain of death; he knew Maya had no money, but there was one way she could earn some cash in a hurry; he hated to ask; did she think she could; oh no, he could never let anyone he loved do that for him; it would only be for a short time, until he paid the "big boys" off, and he would marry her afterward.

Crazy with love, Maya fell for every line of the silver-tongued pimp's rap and agreed to prostitute herself for him. Soon, she was in residence at one of Tolbrook's many houses, where, despite the abundant evidence to the contrary, she was unwilling to believe that her "lover" had betrayed her and that she had fallen for one of the oldest cons in the book. She returned to her senses only after learning that her mother was lying ill in a San Francisco hospital after emergency surgery. She returned home alone via Greyhound, to find her brother awaiting her in her mother's hospital room as well: his wife, Eunice, had died that very day—the first anniversary of their marriage—of tuberculosis. From this blow Bailey would not recover. Heroin reclaimed him; from this point onward he becomes little more than a shadowy presence in Maya's life and literature. Though she never specifies the offenses, other than to point out that his crimes were against property, not persons, it is clear that Bailey—"the person in my family closest to being a genius"—went on to serve several jail sentences. It is perhaps the only aspect of her life that Maya treats with anything less than unflinching honesty in her books—a clear indication of the depth of the pain her brother's fate caused her.

She would soon be made to face certain consequences of her own decisions. With money given her by Bailey for the round-trip, she returned to Stockton to reclaim her child, only to discover that the baby-sitter had vanished, with Clyde. After a day and night of anguish, she succeeded in tracking them down in Bakersfield, nearly 200 miles south; the close call forced upon her the realization that her son was not just some "beautiful appendage" of herself but an individual for whose safety she was responsible.

The wastefulness of her entire recent way of life was further brought home to Maya not long after her return to San Francisco. After taking and then losing an unusual position as the manager of a restaurant in Oakland and chauffeur of the owner's stable of prize-fighters, Maya paid her rent by helping a man named Troubador Martin sell stolen women's clothing. Still looking for love, she grew disappointed when Martin showed no romantic interest in her. It was clear to her that Martin was a junkie, but Maya, who was still smoking marijuana regularly, was even willing to try heroin if that was what it took to attract him. When she pressed Martin about the reason for his disinterest, he took her with him to a shooting gallery and made her watch as he injected heroin and then nodded out. This firsthand exposure to the brutal reality of Troubador's life hit Maya as hard as if she had mainlined the drug herself, and she thought that no man had ever been so kind to her. "No one had ever cared for me so much," she wrote at the end of *Gather Together in My Name*. "He had exposed himself to me to teach me a lesson and I learned it as I sat in the dark car inhaling the odors of the wharf. The life of the underworld was truly a rat race, and

most of its inhabitants scurried like rodents in the sewers and gutters of the world. I had walked the precipice and seen it all; and at the critical moment one man's generosity pushed me safely away from the edge. . . .

"The next day I took the clothes, my bags and Guy back to Mother's. I had no idea what I was going to make of my life, but I had given a promise and found my innocence. I swore I'd never lose it again." ❧

Maya Angelou as she appeared in 1976, at the time of the publication of Singin' and Swingin' and Gettin' Merry Like Christmas, *which chronicles the direction her life took after she resolved to never again lose her innocence.*

7
BECOMING
MAYA ANGELOU

MAYA'S RENEWED DETERMINATION did not immediately make her life any easier. For two years, following her return from Stockton, she and Clyde "spun like water spiders in a relentless eddy." While the mother held down a succession of unfulfilling jobs, often two at a time, her son was boarded out with baby-sitters. The arrangement, which allowed parent and child very little time together, was unsatisfying to both of them, but there seemed to be no immediate solution. At times, Maya hoped to be married, to some man who could provide her and her child with some security and a better way of life, but "there wasn't a shadow of a husband-caliber man on my horizon," she wrote in *Singin' and Swingin' and Gettin' Merry Like Christmas*, the third volume of her memoirs. "Indeed, no men at all seemed attracted to me. Possibly my facade of cool control turned them away or just possibly my need, which I thought well disguised, was so obvious that it frightened them. No, husbands were rarer than common garden variety unicorns."

Welfare was another possibility that was suggested to her, but one that she rejected outright. "Welfare was absolutely forbidden," she wrote. "My pride had been starched by a family who assumed unlimited authority in its own affairs. . . . I hadn't asked them for help, and they loved me. There was no motive on earth which would bring me, bowed, to beg for aid from an institution which scorned me and a government which ignored me."

A scene from George and Ira Gershwin's Porgy and Bess. *Upon seeing a performance of the Gershwins' folk opera, Angelou became "totally consumed" and eventually turned down a spot in a Broadway play for an opportunity to appear in the chorus of* Porgy and Bess.

Her situation eased a bit when she was offered a job in the record store where she bought her beloved jazz and blues disks. She liked the work, exulted in the music she could now listen to all day, and, contrary to expectations, found her white employer to be friendly and without prejudice. ("None of her actions went unheeded, no conversation unrecorded," Maya wrote about Louise Cox, the woman who had befriended her and offered her the job. "The question was not if she would divulge her racism but when and how the revelation would occur. . . . After two months, vigilance had exhausted me and I had found no thread of prejudice.") Feeling more secure about herself, she now accepted her mother's offer of help, and she and her son moved back to Vivian's big house, though she insisted on paying room and board.

But marriage continued to be an appealing fantasy. To Maya, it promised emotional and financial security, freedom from loneliness and economic want. "If I were married," she wrote later about her dreams at this period in her life, "'my husband' (the words sounded as unreal as 'my bank account') would set me up in a fine house, which my good taste would develop into a home. My son and I could spend whole days together and then I could have two more children who would be named Deirdre and Craig, and I would grow roses and beautiful zinnias. I would wear too-large gardening gloves so that when I removed them my hands would look dainty and my manicure fresh. We would all play chess and Chinese checkers and twenty questions and whist."

So when Tosh Angelos, a white, withdrawn, misanthropic sailor of Greek origin who had begun to frequent the record store and court her, asked Maya to marry him, she said yes. Her reasoning, as she explained it to her horrified mother, was simple: "Because he asked me, Mother." Vivian registered her disapproval with a "full-out tantrum" and then by promptly relocating to Los Angeles, and her daughter soon discovered that the reality of her marriage was quite different from the pretty fantasy.

Her husband, who took a job in an electrical appliance store, was "intelligent, kind and reliable" but also opinionated and domineering. Though he loved Maya's son and praised her consistently for her beauty and intelligence, the corollary of his admiration was that few other people in the world met the same standards. Maya was essentially forbidden to have friends and, even more troublesome to her, to attend church services; Tosh was an atheist, and Clyde was to be taught strictly that there was no God. Initially, comforted by the "cocoon of safety" in which Tosh swaddled her and her son, Maya did not object to such restrictions, but she was too independent to tolerate them for long. The ineradicable belief that she was "a child of God" was central to her self-image, and she regarded the church as a defining element of her black heritage that she did not wish to relinquish; she wished as well that Clyde be exposed to some religious experience and began to worry that having a white stepfather might undermine her efforts to develop in her son a sense of pride in his black ancestry. Inevitably, gradually at first and then more quickly, the marriage came apart under the weight of these pressures.

Once again, Maya was on her own, with nowhere to turn. Vivian was in Los Angeles, and Grandmother Henderson had died. At Tosh's insistence, Maya had quit her job at the record store; now, to make ends meet, she took a job as a dancer and bar girl at a strip joint called the Garden of Allah. In this depressing, unlikely setting, her fortune began to change. Part of her duties included hustling men at the bar into buying her drinks; her sassy patter and unorthodox practice of explaining to these men that the drinks were watered down and that she received a percentage of the take soon earned her some notoriety and the club new patrons, as did her uninhibited dancing, clad as Scheherazade, to tunes such as Dizzy Gillespie's "A Night in Tunisia" and Duke Ellington's "Caravan."

Even so, after a few months she was fired; jealous of her popularity, the club's other dancers had charged that her appeal was the result of her sleeping with customers. But among her new fans were entertainers and employees of the Purple Onion, a classy, hip basement nightclub in the city's trendy North Beach section, who told her that the club was looking for a folk singer. Fearless as ever, Maya, despite her total lack of musical experience and training, auditioned as a singer of calypso songs and landed the gig. When the club's management deemed the name Marguerite Johnson to be insufficiently glamorous for its new act, the budding star came up with the stage name Maya Angelou. (Maya, of course, had been Bailey's childhood nickname for her; Angelou was

The Purple Onion was a hip San Francisco nightclub where the performing careers of comedians Phyllis Diller and Mort Sahl, among others, were launched and where Marguerite Johnson, a tall singer and dancer, first used the name Maya Angelou.

an exotic-sounding corruption of her married name of Angelos.)

Maya Angelou's unusual combination of song and dance—when, as often happened, she forgot the lyrics to her long calypso tales, she simply began dancing—made her an immediate star. Soon, she even began composing her own songs by setting the words to poems she had written to music. Her performances attracted the attention of several talent scouts, and after auditioning she landed spots in two Broadway plays and in the touring company of *Porgy and Bess*, George and Ira Gershwin's "folk opera," which had been written for an all-black cast and tells the tale, set among the black denizens of Catfish Row, North Carolina, of the tragic love of Porgy, a crippled black beggar, for the beautiful and unfaithful Bess. With the great soprano Leontyne Price as the female lead, Maya had seen the show performed when the troupe passed through San Francisco and had been devastated by its emotional power. "I went to the theater ready to be entertained," she wrote, "but not expecting a riot of emotion. By intermission I had been totally consumed. I had laughed and cried, exulted and mourned, and expected the second act to produce no new emotions. . . . I was stunned. *Porgy and Bess* had shown me the greatest array of Negro talent I had ever seen."

Her reaction made her choice easy; to the amazement of the Broadway producer who had offered her a major part in his new production, she chose instead a role in the chorus of the international company of *Porgy and Bess*. The only aspect of her decision that was difficult was that going on tour—the company was scheduled to visit 22 nations—meant leaving Clyde for many months. Though he would be well cared for by Vivian Baxter, who had returned to San Francisco and opened a soul-food restaurant, memories of her own periods of separation from her

Leslie Scott (kneeling, at center) played Porgy in the international touring company of Porgy and Bess, *with which Angelou traveled. Scott was as "handsome and as private as an African mask," Angelou wrote.*

mother tormented Maya: "The past revisited. My mother had left me with my grandmother for years and I knew the pain of parting. My mother, like me, had her motivations, her needs. I did not relish visiting the same anguish on my son, and she, years later, had told me how painful our separation was to her." Still, she judged the opportunity worth the heartache that both of them would endure.

The tour took Maya and *Porgy and Bess* to Montreal, Canada; Venice, Italy; Paris, France (where by overwhelming popular demand their scheduled week-long engagement was held over for several months); Zagreb and Belgrade in Yugoslavia; Cairo, Egypt; Athens, Greece; Tel Aviv, Israel; the North African nation of Morocco; Barcelona, Spain; Lausanne,

Switzerland; and Milan, Genoa, Florence, Turin, and Rome in Italy. For the company, the highlight of the trip was their engagement in Milan, where *Porgy and Bess* became the first American opera ever sung on the stage of La Scala, the famous opera house, home to the most sophisticated and demanding opera aficionados in the world. The troupe performed spectacularly, and the audience was generous in its appreciation. For Maya personally, the high point was Paris, where she moonlighted as a nightclub performer to much acclaim.

Everywhere, she was impressed by the dignity and respect with which the company was treated. In a music store in Zagreb, a woman overcame the language barrier by saying the name "Paul Robeson," the great black American singer and actor, and then singing, with great emotion, the spiritual "Deep River, Lord," which she had apparently learned from a Robeson recording. That the experience, suffering, and longing of her own people, as articulated in the words and music of the spiritual, could contain such profound meaning for these foreigners was overwhelming to Maya. At a party elsewhere in Yugoslavia, which was then a communist nation whose citizens' intercourse with the outside world was severely restricted, Maya was stunned when her hosts began playing records by Lester Young, Billie Holiday, Sarah Vaughan, and other jazz greats, whom they went on to speak of with the greatest reverence. The realization that these musicians and vocalists, who received so little respect in their own land, were here recognized as important artists filled her anew with pride in her heritage as a black American.

Such pride was something she had worked hard to instill in her son, and after almost a year abroad, she determined to leave the company and return home to him. Her resolve was made firmer by a letter from her mother informing her that Clyde had de-

The Apollo Theater in Harlem was the most prestigious venue Maya Angelou played as a vocalist. "The Apollo, in Harlem, was to black entertainers the Met, La Scala and a Royal Command Performance combined," Angelou wrote.

veloped a mysterious rash that had proved resistant to all medical treatment. Overjoyed to be reunited with her son, she tortured herself nonetheless for ever having left him, especially when he asked her when she would be leaving again; but together, in time, the two restored to each other a sense of security. With his mother's return, Clyde's rash dried up and soon disappeared, and Maya recognized that the greatest gift she could give her son was herself. In his continuing need for her, coupled with his rapidly developing sense of self—soon after her return, he renamed himself Guy—was the verification she needed of her worth as a mother.

Justification for the sacrifice the two of them had made was soon forthcoming. Although Maya never regarded herself as an especially noteworthy vocalist, in the wake of her *Porgy and Bess* experience her singing career blossomed, as she describes in *The Heart of a Woman*. Regular gigs on the West Coast and in Hawaii (with Guy often accompanying her) led to the economic independence she had long craved, and by the end of the 1950s she was even able to rent a home for herself and her son in the fashionable Laurel Canyon section of Los Angeles, which she thought would be a more suitable city than San Francisco from which to pursue a show business career.

Having scratched so long to secure some semblance of security for herself and Guy, Maya now found it difficult not to seek out new challenges. Her lyric writing led to a renewed interest in composing poetry and even short stories, an interest that was encouraged by John Oliver Killens, a black novelist who had come to the West Coast to write a screenplay. Killens took the time to read some of her work; after explaining that she had "undeniable talent," he urged her to move to New York City and join the Harlem Writers Guild, an informal organization of writers that met regularly to read and con-

structively criticize one another's work. At the urging
of her friend Abbey Lincoln, the jazz singer and
actress, Maya had actually been contemplating such
a move for some time, and Killens's encouragement
was the final incentive she needed. With the fre-
quently uprooted Guy in tow, she set out for New
York, where, in 1959, she settled in Brooklyn.

As if in compensation for the years of scuffling,
good things now began to happen in a hurry for Maya
Angelou. She landed singing gigs at various clubs and
even at the famed Apollo Theater in Harlem, long
the most prestigious venue for black entertainers.
When not singing, she wrote and tested her literary
efforts before the demanding yet well-meaning critics
of the Harlem Writers Guild. There were new and
exciting friendships, especially with Abbey Lincoln
and her husband, the legendary jazz drummer Max
Roach, with the comedian Godfrey Cambridge, and
with various activists in the forefront of the civil
rights movement, foremost among them Bayard Rustin, one of Martin Luther King, Jr.'s most trusted
lieutenants in the Southern Christian Leadership
Conference (SCLC), King's civil rights organization.
With Cambridge, Maya wrote and performed in
Cabaret for Freedom, an off-Broadway revue, featuring
the talents of a number of exciting young artists
and performers, that was produced as a benefit for
the SCLC. The penchant for organization she
demonstrated in that endeavor led to her being
offered a position as Rustin's successor as the north-
ern coordinator for SCLC and a deepening involve-
ment in the civil rights struggle. In this capacity
she met King and the charismatic Malcolm X,
but the most significant of her new acquaintances was
a visiting South African freedom fighter named
Vusumzi Make.

Make had come to New York in 1960 to speak at
the United Nations and drum up support, both moral

In 1960, Angelou (center) appeared as the White Queen in an off-Broadway production of The Blacks, *Jean Genet's daring dramatic indictment of colonial imperialism. Besides Angelou, the production featured an incredible array of African-American talent, including James Earl Jones, Roscoe Lee Browne, Godfrey Cambridge, Cicely Tyson, Louis Gossett, Jr., Abbey Lincoln, and Max Roach.*

and financial, for the struggle against apartheid in his own nation. Upon hearing him speak eloquently about the situation in his homeland, Maya fell deeply and blindly in love. A somewhat serious relationship with a bail bondsman named Thomas quickly fell by the wayside when Make announced his intention to marry her and bring her back to Africa to help him with the struggle for black self-determination. Despite Make's roving eye and an alarming disregard for such details as paying bills—a propensity that resulted in their being evicted from a lavish Central Park West apartment in which he had established them— Maya agreed that she and Guy would go with him. The wisdom of this decision, both for herself and for her now teenaged son, did not greatly concern her. "Whether our new start was going to end in success or failure didn't cross my mind," she wrote in

remembrance many years later. "What I did know. . . was that it was exciting."

Though Make was serious in his devotion to the cause of freedom for the blacks of South Africa, he was an equally dedicated womanizer, and the elegantly appointed apartment in which he settled his new family in Cairo, Egypt—then a kind of international headquarters for African revolutionaries in exile—provided Maya with little sense of security once it became apparent that, as in New York, Make was not overly concerned with how such luxury was to be paid for. Within a short time, creditors began arriving, demanding payment for various items of furniture and other merchandise, and Guy's tuition

Angelou "married" (there was no formal ceremony) the South African freedom fighter Vusumzi Make (left) in 1960. Though she admired Make's commitment to the cause of black liberation in South Africa, Maya would come to regret that her husband did not bring the same dedication to their relationship.

One of the many mosques of Cairo, Egypt. Angelou came to Cairo with Make and her son in 1961, but it was not until she left her husband and moved to Ghana with Guy that she felt that she was experiencing the real Africa.

at school went unpaid for months at a time. Maya also chafed at the various restrictions her new husband placed on her freedom, such as his forbidding her to work. With the help of an American journalist, David DuBois, she took a job anyway, as associate editor of the *Arab Observer* (once again making up in nerve, intelligence, and hard work what she lacked in experience), and in a short time, under the weight of Make's philandering, the marriage broke up.

Maya was determined to remain in Africa. Guy was now 17 and ready for college; Ghana, in West Africa, was reputed to have one of the continent's best universities. Ghana was, moreover, the subject of intense interest on the part of many black Americans, as it was one of the first nations of black Africa to have obtained its independence from European colonial rule following World War II. Its premier, Kwame Nkrumah, was regarded as a hero by many blacks, and he had let it be known that American blacks who were interested in working for the cause of African independence or in returning to their roots were welcome in Ghana. Nkrumah had demonstrated the sincerity of his offer by providing a home in his nation for the elderly W. E. B. Du Bois, civil rights leader, founder of the National Association for the Advancement of Colored People (NAACP), and arguably the foremost black American intellectual of the 20th century. For all his achievements, Du Bois had long been targeted by the U.S. government for harassment, and he was proud to make his last home in a nation where blacks controlled their own economic and political destiny.

For Maya, the prospect of becoming a member of the small colony of expatriate black Americans in Ghana thus held great appeal. "Since we were descendants of African slaves torn from the land," she wrote in *All God's Children Need Traveling Shoes*, the last volume, to date, of her autobiography, "we reasoned we wouldn't have to earn the right to return, yet we wouldn't be so arrogant as to take anything for granted. We would work and produce, then snuggle down into Africa as a baby nuzzles in a mother's arms." Maya and Guy settled in Accra, Ghana's capital, where, after recovering from severe injuries suffered in an automobile accident, Guy enrolled at the University of Ghana. His mother took a job at the university as an administrative assistant; she also continued her career as a journalist, contributing articles to various Ghanaian publications, and in time she was asked to teach at the university.

At times, the intensity of the feelings she experienced in Ghana overwhelmed Maya. In Egypt, Maya had often felt that she was in a country less African than Arabic, but Ghana was different. Everywhere, it seemed, were reminders of the common kinship that linked blacks in America and in Africa, and of the historical tragedy that had sundered these ancestral relationships. Ghana had been a center of the slave trade; the European commerce in Africans had begun in Portuguese forts established in the 15th century along its coasts. "Here, there, along the banks of that river, someone was taken, tied with ropes, shackled with chains, forced to march for weeks carrying the double burden of neck irons and abysmal fear. In that large clump of trees . . . boys and girls had been hunted like beasts, caught and tethered together. . . . Every ill I knew at home, each hateful look on a white face, each odious rejection based on skin color, the mockery, the disenfranchisement, the lamentations and loud wailing for a lost world, irreclaimable security, all that long onerous journey to misery, which had not ended yet, had begun [here]."

There were joyful recognitions as well. To her surprise, much of what she saw in Ghana reminded Maya of her childhood in Stamps. "I was captured by the Ghanaian people," she wrote in *All God's Children Need Traveling Shoes*. "Their skins were the color of my childhood cravings: peanut butter, licorice, chocolate and caramel. Theirs was the laughter of home, quick and without artifice. The erect and graceful walk of the women reminded me of my Arkansas grandmother, Sunday-hatted, on her way to church. I listened to men talk, and whether or not I understood their meaning, there was a melody as familiar as sweet potato pie, reminding me of my Uncle Tommy Baxter in Santa Monica, California."

In Ghana, she discovered in a short time, there was no need to gird herself against the kind of racial prejudice that was an everyday experience in the United States, and she felt a tremendous sense of freedom. "I loved Ghana," she told an interviewer in 1974. "It was the first time I ever felt at home in my life. When I was three years old, I was sent from California to Arkansas with an identification tag

around my neck. . . . Until I was thirteen, when I left Arkansas, I was known as Mrs. Henderson's California granddaughter. When I went back to California, I was called the Southern girl. And when I went to New York to study dance, I was the tall girl from California. Wherever I went, I belonged somewhere else. But in Ghana, I was called the child who has returned home."

The culmination of this sense of homecoming came in the marketplace of the coastal village of Keta in 1965, near the end of Maya's stay in Ghana. Upon seeing Maya, an elderly woman there grew extremely agitated and began trying desperately to communicate something to the stranger from America. Maya herself was very moved by the woman's appearance, for "she had the wide face and slanted eyes of my

Kwame Nkrumah (right, in white suit), the first president of independent Ghana, was a hero to many black Americans for his role in leading his nation to independence.

Among Angelou's many highly regarded dramatic performances on stage and screen was her appearance (rear) in the 1977 television miniseries Roots.

grandmother. Her lips were large and beautifully shaped like those of my grandmother's, and her cheek bones were high like those of my grandmother." Maya did not understand Ewe, the language the woman was speaking, but she got someone to translate.

"This is a very sad story and I can't tell it all or tell it well," said the interpreter in explaining what the woman, who had been joined by several of her equally demonstrative friends, was trying to communicate. At one point during the slave era, Keta had been overrun by slave traders. During one especially tragic raid, virtually "every inhabitant was killed or taken." The only ones to escape were some children, who "watched from their hiding places as their parents were beaten and put into chains. They saw the slaves traders set fire to the village. They saw mothers and fathers take infants by their feet and bash their heads against tree trunks rather than see them sold into slavery. What they saw they remembered and what they remembered they told over and over." The orphaned children were taken in by the people of another village; in time, they married, and they and their descendants rebuilt Keta. Always, the story of what had happened to their ancestors was handed down, from generation to generation, in the oral tradition of West Africa.

"These women are the descendants of those orphaned children," her translator told Maya. "They have heard the stories often, and the deeds are still as fresh as if they had happened during their lifetimes. And you, Sister, you look so much like them, even the tone of your voice is like theirs. They are sure you are descended from those stolen mothers and fathers." The women now were weeping, mourning "not for you but for their lost people." Maya joined them in their tears.

But having "continually and accidentally tripped" over "the roots of [her] beginnings" in Ghana, Maya nevertheless came to realize that Africa, no matter how much she had come to love it, was not her home. Her story had begun there, long ago, perhaps in the very way told her by the women in the marketplace, but history can only be understood, never undone. Maya, as she now deeply understood, was an American, and it was time to return home.

The nation she was returning to was no less troubled than when she had left, particularly on the issue of equal rights for its black citizens. Several days after her return, Malcolm X, from whom she had accepted a position as coordinator for his Organization of Afro-American Unity, was assassinated. Three years later, Martin Luther King, Jr., was also murdered. With its two most eloquent voices stilled, the civil rights movement lost much of its momentum, and America's promise of equality of opportunity for all its citizens remains unfulfilled.

But life lies in the struggle, Maya's experience had taught her, and neither personal nor historical tragedies could long hold her or her people down. In Keta, she wrote at the conclusion of *All God's Children Need Traveling Shoes*, she had cried "for all the lost people, their ancestors and mine," but she had wept "with a curious joy. Despite the murders, rapes and suicides, we had survived. The middle passage and the auction block had not erased us. Not humiliations nor lynchings, individual cruelties nor collective oppression had been able to eradicate us from the earth. . . . There was much to cry for, much to mourn, but in my heart I felt exalted knowing there was much to celebrate . . . [for] we had dared to continue to live. . . . Through the centuries of despair and dislocation, we had been creative, because we had dared to hope."

Her experience in Africa is the end, thus far, of the remarkable story that Maya Angelou has been able to bring herself to remember. Her legacy of achievements and honors since is remarkable—four published volumes of poetry in addition to the five volumes of autobiography; several produced screenplays and teleplays; membership as the first black woman in the Directors Guild; Tony and Emmy awards nominations for dramatic performances on Broadway and on television; numerous honorary degrees and awards; professorships at several universities—but it is her life and its telling that stands as the best record of Maya Angelou's own infinite capacity for daring, hope, and creativity. Today, she is a professor at Wake Forest University in North Carolina, where she brings all of her enthusiasm and knowledge to the attempt to instill in her students what she regards as the simple message of her life and work: "That I am a human being; nothing human can be alien to me . . . that we are all of us more alike than unalike. . . . [that] it is love that holds us together as human beings." She continues in her unending quest to lead a "poetic life," one lived "fully, fiercely, devotedly" and characterized by hard work, wisdom, love, and especially courage, "the most important of all the virtues because without it one cannot practice

any other virtue with consistency." For young black men and women, she preaches the means of her own salvation: reading, especially African-American literature. "It is for your security," she explained to her students in 1987. "It tells you, implicitly and explicitly: someone was here before you, and survived it. The minute you start to inject this literature, something happens to the spirit. It lifts. You pick yourself up, dust yourself off, and prepare to love somebody. I don't mean sentimentality. I mean the condition of the human spirit so profound that it encourages us to build bridges."

"One of the first things that a young person must internalize, deep down in the blood and bones, is the understanding that although he may encounter many defeats, he must not be defeated. If life teaches us anything, it may be that we need to suffer some defeats."

CHRONOLOGY

1928   Born Marguerite Johnson on April 4 in St. Louis, Missouri

1931   With brother Bailey, sent to live with grandmother in Stamps, Arkansas

1940   Graduates from Lafayette County Training School; moves to San Francisco to live with her mother

1944   Works as a conductor on San Francisco cable cars

1945   Graduates from Mission High School; her son Guy is born

1952   Marries Tosh Angelos

1953   Performs at the Purple Onion nightclub in San Francisco; adopts stage name Maya Angelou

1954–55   Tours internationally with the Everyman's Opera Company production of *Porgy and Bess*

1959   Moves to Brooklyn, New York, to join the Harlem Writers Guild

1960   Selected as northeastern regional coordinator for Southern Christian Leadership Conference; appears in off-Broadway play, *The Blacks*; produces, directs, and performs in *Cabaret for Freedom*

1961–62   Marries South African freedom fighter Vusumzi Make and moves to Africa; becomes associate editor for *Arab Observer* in Cairo, Egypt

1963–65   Serves as assistant administrator at the School of Music and Drama, University of Ghana; feature editor for the *African Review*; and contributor to the *Ghanaian Times* and Ghanaian Broadcasting Company

1970   First book of autobiography, *I Know Why the Caged Bird Sings,* is published and nominated for National Book Award; is writer-in-residence at University of Kansas; granted Yale University fellowship

1971   *Just Give Me a Cool Drink of Water 'Fore I Diie,* her first volume of poetry, is published

1972   Nominated for Pulitzer Prize; *Georgia, Georgia* screenplay is produced

1973   Receives Tony nomination for acting in *Look Away;* marries Paul Du Feu

1974   *Gather Together in My Name* is published; becomes distinguished visiting professor at Wake Forest University, Wichita State University, and California State University

1975	*Oh Pray My Wings Are Gonna Fit Me Well*, a collection of poems, is published
1976	*Singin' and Swingin' and Gettin' Merry Like Christmas* is published; selected as Woman of the Year in communications by *Ladies' Home Journal*
1978	*And Still I Rise*, a book of poems, is published
1981	*The Heart of a Woman* is published
1982	Appointed chair in American Studies at Wake Forest University, North Carolina; writes *Sister, Sister* for NBC
1983	Publishes collection of poems, *Shaker, Why Don't You Sing?*
1986	*All God's Children Need Traveling Shoes* is published
1990	*I Shall Not Be Moved*, a collection of poems, is published
1993	At the new president's request, reads her poem "On the Pulse of Morning" at the inauguration of Bill Clinton

FURTHER READING

Angelou, Maya. *All God's Children Need Traveling Shoes*. New York: Random House, 1986.

———. *And Still I Rise*. New York: Random House, 1978.

———. *Gather Together in My Name*. New York: Random House, 1974.

———. *The Heart of a Woman*. New York: Random House, 1981.

———. *I Know Why the Caged Bird Sings*. New York: Random House, 1970.

———. *Just Give Me a Cool Drink of Water 'Fore I Diie*. New York: Random House, 1971.

———. *Now Sheba Sings the Song*. New York: Dutton, 1987.

———. *Oh Pray My Wings Are Gonna Fit Me Well*. New York: Random House, 1978.

———. *Shaker, Why Don't You Sing?* New York: Random House, 1983.

———. *Singin' and Swingin' and Gettin' Merry Like Christmas*. New York: Random House, 1976.

Elliot, Jeffrey M., ed. *Conversations with Maya Angelou*. Jackson: University of Mississippi Press, 1989.

INDEX

PICTURE CREDITS

MILES SHAPIRO is a Yale University graduate whose short stories, essays, and book reviews have appeared in various publications. He is the author of *Bill Russell* in Chelsea House's BLACK AMERICANS OF ACHIEVEMENT series. A native of Washington, D.C., he currently resides in Brooklyn, New York.

NATHAN IRVIN HUGGINS, one of America's leading scholars in the field of black studies, helped select the titles for the BLACK AMERICANS OF ACHIEVEMENT series, for which he also served as senior consulting editor. He was the W.E.B. Du Bois Professor of History and of Afro-American Studies at Harvard University and the director of the W.E.B. Du Bois Institute for Afro-American Research at Harvard. He received his doctorate from Harvard in 1962 and returned there as a professor in 1980 after teaching at Columbia University, the University of Massachusetts, Lake Forest College, and the California State University, Long Beach. He was the author of four books and dozens of articles, including *Black Odyssey: The Afro-American Ordeal in Slavery*, *The Harlem Renaissance*, and *Slave and Citizen: The Life of Frederick Douglass*, and was associated with the Children's Television Workshop, National Public Radio, the Boston Athenaeum, the Museum of Afro-American History, the Howard Thurman Educational Trust, and Upward Bound. Professor Huggins died in 1989, at the age of 62, in Cambridge, Massachusetts.